Who Are You Calling a Widow?

A Memoir of Love, Loss and Self-Discovery

10/13/19

To Anthony,
My new best bud. Happy
reading. Thank you for your
support.

Love,

Amelia Peg

Who Are You Calling a Widow?

A Memoir of Love, Loss and Self-Discovery

ANDREA PEREZ

Yellow Ribbon Publishing
2019

ISBN: 9781099041624

Library of Congress Control Number 2019906747

Printed in the United States of America

AndreaPerez.net

DEDICATION

*For those who have lost someone,
and in turn lost themselves.*

*For my fellow military widows —
May your love for your spouse and your country
give you the strength to pursue happiness
each and every day.*

"Happiness can be found,
even in the darkest of times,
if one only remembers to turn on the light."

– J. K. Rowling

CONTENTS

Preface

Introduction

Chapter 1	Young Love	1
Chapter 2	Hurry Up and Wait	13
Chapter 3	Tragic News	29
Chapter 4	Gasping for Air	39
Chapter 5	Saying Goodbye	51
Chapter 6	A Final Salute	67
Chapter 7	My Last Visit to Fort Polk	79
Chapter 8	The Widow	87
Chapter 9	Going Through the Motions	97
Chapter 10	Breaking Point	113
Chapter 11	New Beginnings	121
Chapter 12	(Un)happy Anniversary	133
Chapter 13	Overcoming the Firsts	147

Chapter 14   Moving Forward   161

Chapter 15   Baby Steps   171

Chapter 16   New Freedom   179

Chapter 17   Following My Heart   189

Chapter 18   Reality Check   199

Chapter 19   Signs and Second Chances   207

Afterword   219

Dumb Shit People Say   223

Acknowledgments   229

Military Support Foundations   233

About the Author   237

PREFACE

Given my yearning for privacy, many were surprised when they found out I was writing a book. To be honest, I was just as surprised. Being thrown in the spotlight while grieving caused me to hide away in the shadows and isolate myself from people. I have come a long way. Sharing my story is one of the scariest things I have done and has helped me grow in ways I could never have imagined.

I needed to make something good come from something so horrible. To help others who can understand the depths of grief and also light a candle of hope to those who could use it. I want to allow my pain to make a difference in someone's life and to show people they are not alone. Maybe my story won't make a difference in your life. And that's okay. Maybe it will help you find out more about what military families face, to learn about an incredible hero, and to realize that life is precious, difficult and beautiful. Because life is not meant to be easy, and we all face some type of struggle. It's when overcome the difficulties that you get to enjoy the true beauty in this world.

Who Are You Calling a Widow? is a true story. I started journaling as a form of therapy to not forget the past. Several entries grew from present-day situations and some took me many years to complete. This is how I remember these events. When I couldn't remember the exact details of some moments, I relied on friends and family who were there to help me with those details. Some names are changed to protect their privacy, while others granted me their consent to use their real names. It is not possible to remember every exact detail without filtering or slightly embellishing. This is the truth as I remember it. I have told my story to the best of my ability and as accurately as possible. There are many things I have left out. While I am sharing so much of my life during that time, there are also things that are meant to be kept private.

ANDREA PEREZ

ROCKLAND COUNTY, NEW YORK, 2019

INTRODUCTION

Widow. This is the word that haunts me. That stalks me. I'm no longer a wife, friend, daughter, or sister. I'm not even Andrea. Widow is what I am. It's what defines me. I'm another number to add to the statistic. An outlier, as I was widowed at age twenty-five, not eighty-five. Regardless of age, it's a classification no one wants. It's one that's forced upon us whether we're prepared for it or not.

Through the seemingly endless process of filling out paperwork, I also discovered another label for what I am. Surviving Spouse. An odd term, I think. What did I survive? I wasn't in Afghanistan. I didn't survive a car crash or cancer or a freak accident. And in truth, I don't feel like I survived. Survival implies a triumph over an obstacle or a miraculous recovery after an illness. Those individuals are survivors.

I didn't survive so much as I persisted. My most vital organ—my heart—broke in a way that no surgeon or medication could possibly repair. Nor is there any proven cure for the emotional and mental bruises I sustained. These internal scars will be with me forever. Instead of Surviving Spouse, it should be B. A. B., for Brokenhearted, Alone, and Bitter. Then again, maybe Surviving Spouse is preferable to Widow. At least I'm still considered a spouse.

I lost my husband and myself on the same day. But this isn't a story about being a widow—at least, not entirely. It's the story of how I became Andrea again.

Chapter One

YOUNG LOVE

True love.

Two little words that carry immeasurable weight. Some are fortunate enough to find it, while others search for it fruitlessly their entire lives. True love is a treasure and once you have it, you'll do anything you can to keep it. Believe me. I would have gone to the ends of the earth to get Eddie back.

My story begins on a beautiful December night in New York City. The weather was cool but not freezing like it usually was that time of year. My friend Christine and I had dinner and drinks at a small, trendy restaurant. Being a true city girl, she has a knack for finding the newest hotspots. The restaurant held an ostentatious chandelier in the center while dimmed lights ran parallel across the wall, giving it a romantic and elegant feel. We've been friends since our freshman year of high school, and ten years later, we still found time in our busy schedules for each other.

As girl-talk normally does, it didn't take long for our conversation to turn to our relationships.

"How did you know that you wanted to marry Eddie?" Christine asked.

I wasn't surprised by the question—I knew she loved her boyfriend, but I also knew she struggled with the feeling there was something missing in the relationship. I wanted to be truthful, but I also wanted to provide her with answers.

"I just knew," I replied. "In past relationships, there was always something absent. There was always a *but*. I like him *but* I don't feel like he's motivated, I like him *but* we're not really connecting. When I met Eddie, it was as if we'd been waiting for each other. Everything made sense. He was everything I ever wanted in a man, and I knew I had to spend the rest of my life with him. I thought I'd been in love before, but after meeting Eddie I finally learned what true love felt like. The kind of feeling where no matter what's happening, everything is right in the world when you are with that other person."

Lost in whatever thoughts my words triggered, Christine took another sip of her drink. Everything I told her was the truth. Even though I was scared about Eddie being in the military, I knew nothing would keep us from being together. Initially, I needed a little convincing from Eddie to believe a long-distance relationship could work, but he changed my mind with his absolute faith in us.

Christine continued chewing on my words, as I reflected on a few years earlier at SUNY Cortland, where I'd met my future husband. It was spring semester of 2006, and we'd both transferred at the same time. Eddie loved telling the story of how we met, cherishing the detail about exactly what I was wearing that day. Black Cortland sweatpants and a grey, zip-up hoodie—boring but typical, college clothing. Before we were even a couple, it seemed we were already dressing alike.

Having transferred to Cortland during the second semester of my junior year, it was a challenge to make close friends. I had people to hang out with, but lacked a deep connection. My roommates were great, but we didn't share similar schedules. I missed my friends from SUNY Oneonta and, I'll admit, was a little too desperate for company.

The day I met Eddie, I was having lunch at the food court with a guy friend from one of my classes. He was self-involved—definitely not my type—but nice enough, and I didn't feel like eating alone. By sheer coincidence, he happened to be on the rugby team with Eddie and was also a member of the fraternity he was pledging. We grabbed our food and he suggested we sit at a table already occupied by Eddie and his roommate, John.

John was a tall, handsome guy who greeted me warmly. Eddie was seated next to him. My first impression was of beautiful blue eyes, a huge smile, sandy brown hair, and a muscular build. He was wearing sweats and a hoodie, just like me and most of the other students in the cafeteria. It was the standard school "uniform" for our cold winters. The ground outside was covered in snow, and the wind chill felt like it could give you frostbite in seconds.

After meeting Eddie and John, I remember thinking, *Wow, nice, laid-back guys do go here.* As

Cortland is a big Physical Education college, a lot of the men put off tough-guy vibes. Eddie was in a different class. He seemed genuine, sweet, and his smile lit up the room. After I left lunch that day, I kept thinking about Eddie and his roommate. They were the type of people I wanted to spend time with. Nice and down to earth.

That Friday night, my roommates and I went to a popular frat house nicknamed the Castle. It was a huge, old, rustic building that actually did resemble a castle. As soon as we walked in, however, the stench of stale beer and sticky floors assaulted us. It was a great place to meet a variety of people, and don't get me wrong, I really liked a lot of them, but it just wasn't my crowd. Being that we had different interests, I didn't really fit into their world.

That night, Eddie was there. When I saw him, I was so excited, and from the smile on his face, I knew he was just as excited to see me. We only spoke for a little while before my roommates whisked me away, but the conversation was great. When he asked for my number, I didn't hesitate to give it to him. It was nice to talk to someone who was on the same level as me. Transfer students making a new beginning.

The following night, my roommates and I were hanging out in our suite getting ready to go out again. Eddie texted, asking me what I was up to and I jumped at the chance to invite him to join us. He accepted and when he arrived, he walked in like we'd been friends forever, exuding confidence and maturity. Everyone else was preoccupied with their own conversations, so Eddie and I went to my room to chat. We talked about the schools we transferred from and our friends there, and found out we had something interesting in common. We'd both left our old schools even though we didn't want to. I left Oneonta because I changed majors, and he left St. John Fisher because it benefited him financially to switch to a state school. Such a small coincidence, but it felt like more. It felt like I'd finally met someone who understood me. We just clicked.

We hung out several more times as friends, but just a few weeks later, things between us changed. It was the birthday of Eddie and one of my suitemates, so a bunch of us went out for sushi to celebrate. We had a great time and afterward went back to my suite to continue celebrating their birthdays by pumping up the music and enjoying some drinks. We were all together in the common room, but little by little, everyone started going to bed. I was getting ready to call it a night, too. I was so tired my contacts felt like they were sticking to my eyes. I went to take them out and returned wearing my dorky glasses. Eddie immediately commented on how cute I looked. I figured either he actually liked them, or he was being sweet and lying to me to make me feel less dorky. At the prospect of hanging out with him longer, I suddenly wasn't tired anymore.

Some time later, we were sitting on a couch together watching a silly show on MTV called *Yo Momma*, where people have to compete for the title of best yo-momma joke. By this point, everyone was asleep in the rooms, though one of my roommates had fallen asleep on another couch in the common area. Eddie and I joked and laughed together quietly. Jumping on any excuse to touch him, I playfully pushed his shoulder every time he made me laugh.

I really wanted to kiss him, but I didn't want to make the first move. My thoughts were a jumble. *Will he kiss me? Wow, I really like this guy. I really want to kiss him.* Finally, we quieted and made eye contact. Eddie gave me the sweetest, most adoring look and next thing I knew, his lips were touching mine. It was, in a word, perfect.

Then, from the other couch, my sleeping roommate yelled, "YO MOMMA!" Stunned, Eddie and I broke apart, only to see my roommate was still completely asleep. She must have been dreaming she was on the show.

We laughed for what felt like twenty minutes straight. Eddie then carried my roommate to her bed. When he returned, we stayed in the common room for a little longer, laughing, kissing, and talking. It was very late when he gave me a goodnight kiss and left my dorm room. I watched him walk down the hall. He glanced back several times, smiling from ear to ear. I knew it matched my own smile.

I'd never liked a guy this much so early on and it was a bit scary. I tried to tell myself to stop thinking about him, and that I couldn't possibly like him this much already, but it was no use. I was hooked.

*   *   *

When Eddie and I met at the end of April, we only had a few more weeks left of school. I knew I wanted to get to know him better, but our personal lives were complicated. I was still talking to an ex-boyfriend and Eddie had just gotten out of a relationship. I had deep feelings for Eddie but was also confused.

We went out several times before we returned to our respective hometowns for the summer. He was from Syracuse, New York, and I was in Rockland County, three-and-a-half hours away. Our relationship—if we could even call it that—was still new and the distance between us complicated things further. We spoke several times over the coming months, but they were casual conversations. He mentioned coming to visit, but although I wanted to see him, I was still conflicted. But despite my reservations, I was looking forward to the fall semester and seeing if that obvious connection between us would flourish.

My plans were derailed when, at the end of the summer, Eddie called me and said he wasn't going back to Cortland. He decided to join the Army for a five-year commitment. It was something he always thought about doing. He wanted to serve his country and better his future. When he told me, my heart sank and a lump formed in my throat. I didn't know much about the military, but I figured that his enlistment meant we wouldn't work out. I wondered if I could try a long-distance relationship. This felt extreme and not to mention scary.

Eddie on the other hand was enthusiastic. He explained that it was something that he always wanted to do and that it would better his future. Enlisting would open up numerous opportunities for him. I didn't try to talk him out of it. I respected him for making the decision and going after what he wanted. Over the next couple of months, we only spoke occasionally and as friends.

When I went back to school, I started seeing my ex again. When Eddie found out I was back together with him, he was hurt but also understood. Being in a relationship with one person while harboring feelings for another was new territory for me. I tried not to think about Eddie but I couldn't help it. *What was so different about him? Why couldn't I stop thinking about him?*

Then, two months later, my boyfriend and I broke up again. This time for good. As soon as Eddie found out, he pursued me with conviction. With him back in my life, all of my feelings for him immediately resurfaced. Being with him felt so right—I was a goner. He had a way of making me feel special, like I was the only person in a crowded room. He was the happiest, most easygoing man I ever met, and his optimistic view of the world amazed me. Not to mention, he had a knack for making me laugh. He visited me as much as he could before he had to leave in November to Fort Benning in Georgia for basic training. During those visits, we picked up right where we left off. As November rapidly approached, he asked me if he could write to me. I happily said "yes, of course!"

I was thrilled to get his letters over the following months. I felt like I was in the 1940s, waiting for word to come from my soldier overseas. Obsessing over checking the mailbox became a part of my routine. I even sent him a package for Thanksgiving, not knowing that he was required to do pushups for every package he received. The drill sergeants thoroughly enjoyed the candy and treats intended for him. But Eddie just laughed about it and told me how much he looked forward to receiving my letters. A couple of times he was able to sneak away and call me. Those surprise phone calls were always exciting.

When he finally got out of basic training, he made a beeline directly to me. Spending time together face-to-face was such a gift. We were always laughing, giddy to finally be together. Sadly, the fun only lasted a week before he had to go back to Fort Benning. By then, it was obvious we were crazy about each other. But a part of me was growing more and more nervous at the idea of him being in the military. I never understood people who pursued relationships with soldiers while knowing the many pitfalls that life entailed. Granted, this was long before I knew anything about the military and I soon realized you can't help who you fall in love with.

While Eddie was at Fort Benning, we spoke on the phone often, but I was still hesitant to claim the title of *girlfriend* without assurances that our relationship would work. Eddie was gone for a couple of weeks that time, and I missed him a lot. He wanted to see me but money was really tight, so he couldn't afford a plane ticket. But as I was coming to learn, not much stopped Eddie from going after what he wanted.

In March, he decided to take advantage of a Friday off, rented a car, and drove twelve hours to Cortland to visit me for the weekend. I absolutely couldn't wait to see him. I cleaned my room fifty times while my roommates made fun of me. I didn't care. My sister was also attending Cortland and was excited to meet the guy she heard so much about. Time crawled as I paced my room, nervously waiting. I glanced at the clock so often I wondered if it was broken. The minute hand didn't seem to be moving. Likewise, my phone mocked me, each passing minute feeling like an hour.

Finally, at two o'clock in the morning, Eddie pulled into the driveway. I ran out the door and he met me, lifting me into a tight embrace. He'd just driven twelve hours but didn't complain once, telling me that he would do it again and again just to see me. I couldn't believe it. I felt so special. The weekend was wonderful but went by way too fast. We spent a whole day in bed, talking and laughing. I couldn't get enough of him.

The long talks we had proved to me that we could make our relationship work. I knew Eddie would do whatever it took to be with me. His faith in us was astounding. Quite simply, Eddie wasn't like any guy I had ever met. I knew I wanted him in my life. The closer we grew, the more resolve I had. He was the man I wanted and had been looking for, and, like him, I was going to do whatever it took to make this work.

*   *   *

Following that pivotal weekend, Eddie visited as often as he could. Before long though, he was sent to Fort Polk in Louisiana. The closest city to him with a direct flight was Houston, Texas. After a few weeks we decided to meet there. I'd never been to Texas before, and I was extremely excited to see Eddie and explore. He knew deployment was in his future and we wanted to see each other as much as we could before then. We had another electrifying weekend together, wandering around Houston and visiting the downtown aquarium. As we walked, I held the prize Eddie had proudly won for me playing one of the carnival games. The day was filled with stories and laughter and ended with a romantic dinner. We couldn't stop gazing at each other, and I don't think we stopped smiling for one minute that weekend. Leaving him was extremely difficult.

Our relationship progressed, and every time Eddie had an extended weekend, he flew to New York to see me. For his two-week R&R (Rest and Recuperation), he enticed me to come with him to visit his family in California. I had never been to California before, so the trip west was new and thrilling. To my relief, his parents and siblings welcomed me with open arms. Although I'd met his mother once before, in Chittenango, New York, it was my first time meeting his dad, sister, and brother.

In the months following, I met several of Eddie's closest friends, among them Michael "Finny" Finnegan. At that point, I'd heard so many colorful stories about his and Eddie's time at St. John Fisher that I felt like we were already friends. Spending time with him only cemented the idea. He was everything Eddie had described and more with his funny, outgoing personality and friendly smile. I once again heard the hilarious retelling of how they met.

They had met through Eddie's roommate, and it actually was anything but instant love. Eddie's impression of Finny was that he was weird and arrogant with the way he wore his hat backward, low and over his eyebrows. Toward the end of his first semester, Eddie got sick from food poisoning and found himself prisoner to the community bathroom. Too weak to move, Eddie's roommate found Finny and they carried Eddie back to his room. In the morning, Finny came to check on the aftermath and as soon as he walked in, Eddie gave him a huge smile and opened his arms looking for a hug.

It was nothing but true love after that.

*   *   *

As the days grew colder, my apprehension grew. November was right around the corner, and Eddie would be deploying to Iraq in just a few weeks. I feared for his safety, worried about not being able to see him for months at a time, and terrified for all the unknowns deployment entailed. About a week and a half before he had to leave, he visited me a final time. This was it. The moment we were dreading. I'll never forget how nervous he was when he told me he'd understand if I didn't want to wait for him. His eyes radiated sadness and fear. But there wasn't a doubt in my mind that I wanted to be with him. I immediately assured him of how much I loved him, and that I would be waiting for him to get off the plane next summer. He was elated, kissing me over and over, holding me as tightly as he could. We stood together for a long time, and eventually he directed my attention out the window to the big, beautiful moon.

"You know what's pretty amazing?" he asked. "Even being so far apart, we could be looking at the same thing at exactly the same time."

Chapter Two

HURRY UP AND WAIT

I learned quickly that the deployment of a loved one is an extremely difficult time. I was always nervous and kept my phone charged and with me at all times. The first month was especially challenging because Eddie's unit was undergoing extensive training and phone calls were rare. After that first month, communication improved. There were times he called me every day, while other times a couple of days would pass between conversations. No matter what difficulties he was going through, Eddie always sounded upbeat and eager to talk.

Once a week, I sent him packages. The post office staff now knew me by name. I would gather essential items like deodorant, toothpaste, snacks, coffee, and notes. Putting together the packages helped keep me busy, which is what I needed more than anything. I'd finished college in December, and before my graduation ceremony, he made sure to call and tell me how proud he was. While he wasn't there physically, I felt him close. Even with the distance between us, he always supported me and encouraged me to pursue my goals. After graduation, I was working full time as a technician for an ophthalmologist and living back at home to save money. I still spent a lot of time visiting friends on campus. They helped take my mind off the constant worry I felt for Eddie. But no matter how many friends surrounded me, I was still lonely. I missed Eddie terribly and counted down the days until his return.

Eddie was told his two week R&R would most likely be in June, but June came and went, as did July. As the days wore into weeks, I felt like I was jumping out of my skin. My need to see him was excruciating and dominated my thoughts morning and night. Even though we Skyped often and I was able to see that big beautiful smile of his, it just wasn't the same as being *with* him. Finally, he told me he'd be coming home in September. Having an end in sight was a relief, and for the first time in my life I couldn't wait for summer to be over. With the leaves falling, my soldier was coming home.

I hadn't seen Eddie in person in an agonizingly long ten months. As the final days ticked by, I was barraged by anxious questions in my mind. *Will he be the same as when he left? Will he still love me?* But on the day he was due to arrive, I woke up smiling. The unanswered questions were gone and all I knew was that I was going to be reunited with my love.

I awoke on that beautiful September morning, feeling carefree. I was floating. Everything seemed brighter and happier. I changed my clothes about twenty times and made sure every strand of hair was perfectly in place. I tried desperately to ignore the huge pimple erupting on my chin. I failed, of course, and kept picking at it, which only made it worse. *My first pimple in months and it had to happen today. Not fair!* I covered it up with makeup the best I could, but it was like throwing a bucket of water on a live volcano. I consoled myself with the thought that Eddie wouldn't notice the zit because he'd be staring at the cute sundress I bought for the occasion.

I wore a path in the carpet from pacing, so I decided to escape the confines of my house. I arrived at the airport an hour early and settled in to wait. Finally, Eddie's plane landed and I stood with everyone else, smiling so hard my face hurt. Little by little, the passengers emerged to descend the stairs. From my vantage point, I saw feet before faces. All different kinds of shoes walked down the stairs, from heels to flip-flops to boots. But the boots I was concerned with were the tan, military variety.

What felt like hundreds of shoes later, I saw a pair of combat boots and my heart began pounding in my chest. But it was a false alarm. The legs and waist didn't belong to my soldier. Only minutes later, however, I saw another pair of tan boots and this time, I knew they belonged to Eddie. My heart started racing again as bit by bit, the rest of him was revealed. Legs in camouflage pants, then his waist, arms, and chest, and finally that beautiful smile that I missed so much. My soldier was home.

As soon as he saw me, Eddie ran forward with open arms. He picked me up and swung me around, his lips sealed against mine. It was pure magic, a feeling impossible to describe. Even though we spent ten months apart, in that moment it felt like he never left. We were exactly where we should be. I could no longer imagine life without this incredible man.

*   *   *

While Eddie was deployed, I painstakingly planned a camping trip for his R&R to celebrate his two-week homecoming. What I didn't tell him was that I invited his friends from home and school and I couldn't wait to surprise him. My parents owned a small, isolated parcel of land in rural Monticello, New York, deep in the woods and far from civilization. The location was a great spot for camping. Eddie knew about the trip but thought it was going to be the two of us, my sister Diana, and her boyfriend. When we all arrived, Diana and I stalled by taking our time getting our things out of the car and setting up. We told the guys the tent needed to be set up right away while we still had daylight. As they got to work, Diana and I unloaded the food, kerosene lamp, drinks and blankets. The campsite already had a fire pit and large deck that my dad built with chairs. We took out the radio and started playing music while Diana kept checking her phone to see how far away everyone was. We told Eddie that some of Diana's friends were dropping by, so when her phone rang, she said she was going to meet them so they could find the campsite.

Eddie was excited that the two of us would be alone for a little while. It was really hard for me to not give away the surprise. He hadn't seen his friends in a long time, and I knew he would be so happy. He wanted to go into the trailer so we could be alone, but I made excuses. I told him I didn't want Diana and her friends to walk in on us, so it would be better if we waited for them to come back before separating from the group. He was understandably impatient but agreed. Minutes later, the ruse paid off.

Five cars rolled up to our campsite and Eddie's friend Finny yelled profanity and waved his arms excitedly while hanging out of the window. Initially Eddie was confused. He thought it was Diana's friend yelling at him. He soon realized all the cars were packed with his friends and his sister. His smile, the smile that I loved, made everything worthwhile.

I'd met some of his friends before, but others I was meeting for the first time. The celebration that day was full of drinking games, antics, and even a mock battle with silly string. When we brought out a cake and all sang *Happy Birthday* to Finny, whose birthday was quickly approaching, you could feel the love in the air. Eddie was on cloud nine. He couldn't believe I managed to pull everything together and keep it a secret. Honestly, I couldn't either. But with the help of his friends, it was a huge success. I was just glad it worked out, and that I was able to show him how much he meant to so many people.

After two amazing weeks, Eddie's R&R quickly ended and I had to take him back to the airport and say goodbye to him once again. Even though it was so hard to watch him leave, I was comforted by the knowledge that there were just a few more months left in his deployment and we would be together again.

But January seemed so far away.

*   *   *

The passage of time is a curious thing. When Eddie and I were together, the minutes flew by at a million miles an hour. Without him, they crawled. As January neared, however, the contrasting states seemed to blend. Each minute was an eternity, but each day merged swiftly into the next.

A friend of mine, Lauren, was also dating a man stationed out of Fort Polk, Louisiana, and currently in Iraq. I was comforted to have someone who understood my feelings and could relate to my situation. Her boyfriend was due back at the same time as Eddie, so we decided to travel together to their homecoming ceremony.

January finally arrived and Lauren and I flew to Louisiana. Our soldiers were due to arrive the following day. That night, I lay in my hotel bed staring at the ceiling. Tomorrow was the day I'd been waiting for—my soldier would be home safe and sound. No matter how hard I tried to relax and sleep, adrenaline wouldn't let me rest. I felt like a kid on Christmas Eve. I was able to doze off for an hour or two, but as soon as the sun rose, Lauren and I hopped out of bed and started getting ready. We just couldn't wait anymore.

We scarfed down breakfast even though we still had hours before their arrival. No matter what we did to keep ourselves busy during the day, time crept by at a snail's pace. Nevertheless, it was also finally on our side. Today, we'd be relieved of the burden of waiting.

The gymnasium where the ceremony was to be held was decorated with Welcome Home banners and signs. Mothers, fathers, spouses and kids gathered in a buzz of excitement. As the gym began to fill, someone turned on a large screen in the middle of the floor. Mariah Carey's *Hero* started playing as background to a video of the soldiers coming off the plane. There wasn't a dry eye in the place. My gaze was glued to the screen in hopes of seeing Eddie, but I was unable to find him in the sea of faces.

After several minutes, the doors to the gym opened and about a hundred soldiers entered single file, in perfect formation, all with the same dignified, unsmiling expressions. Hats made it difficult to spot any distinguishing features. My heart pounded hard as I anxiously searched for Eddie.

When all the soldiers were inside, the general approached the podium and said a few words. I honestly can't remember what was said. I was barely listening. I was a kid with someone waving candy in front of my face but telling me I couldn't have it. Thankfully, the general only spoke for a few minutes and then gave the order for the soldiers to break formation. I still couldn't spot Eddie.

Chaos erupted as everyone began running to find their loved ones. Lauren and her boyfriend were reunited, and all around me I witnessed tearful reunions. As I continued frantically searching for my soldier, I heard Lauren yelling my name from across the room. I knew by her voice that she found Eddie. I looked up and there he was with a big smile and his arms spread open for me. He picked me up and swung me around. Our lips finally touched. Suddenly it didn't feel so much like he was coming home as I was. His arms were my home. I never wanted to let him go. Everything was finally right in the world and my life was complete again. Our emotions collided in a torrent of happiness, love, excitement, and peace.

Left: Eddie returned from deployment in Iraq January 6, 2009.
Right: Army Ball, March 2009

He now had one deployment under his belt and only one more left of his military career. Being that his next deployment wasn't for another two years, I decided to bury those worries in the back of my brain. I wanted to savor every moment with him here, now.

That afternoon, Eddie and I drove to L'Auberge, a casino and resort in Lake Charles, Louisiana. We drove hand in hand, smiling the entire drive. The resort was beautiful, our room opulent. It felt like a dream come true. As we were putting our clothes away, I grabbed the complimentary bathrobes from the closet. Minutes later, a bottle of champagne was delivered by room service.

The moment was too perfect to pass up. Smiling, I looked at Eddie. "Well, we have to make up for missing New Year's Eve. Want to do it now?" He laughed and nodded.

We stood in our robes with the bottle of champagne between us and yelled a countdown from ten to one. He popped the cork and we shouted, "HAPPY NEW YEAR!" Then Eddie pulled me close and we had our New Year's kiss just six days late. Late or not, it was perfect.

We spent the next days attached at the hip. But unfortunately, responsibility came calling. I had to return home for work and Eddie had to work before he could take his two weeks' leave. We weren't apart for long. We divided his leave between visiting his family in California, two nights in Las Vegas, as well as a few in New York. It was pure bliss. After that idyllic period, we went back to flying back and forth from New York to Louisiana on the weekends. We saw each other every few weeks, leaving us broke, but happy. Just like he promised me, we made our long-distance relationship work.

Around Christmas, Eddie was due for another two weeks' leave. I spent the holiday with my family, then Diana and I flew to California to spend some time with Eddie's family. I enjoyed traveling with my sister. We were very close and I wanted her to get to know the Bolens. Plus, Eddie and Diana had developed a strong friendship over the last year. Just as I expected, the Bolens were extremely welcoming. "Momma B" even hung up Christmas stockings for Diana and me.

On the second day of our visit, we planned a wine-tasting trip at Ponte Vineyards in Temecula. Diana and Eddie's sister, Clare, decided to do a little shopping in the morning so Eddie and I could have some time alone at the vineyard. I felt badly about abandoning Diana, but she insisted she was fine. Once the girls left, I spent some time relaxing and playing with the family dog, Fred. Eddie, on the other hand, seemed anxious to get going. I didn't see what the rush was, but I got dressed and we headed out.

21

The short twenty-five-minute drive was beautiful. Eddie and I sang along with the radio while enjoying the scenery. Breathtaking mountains rose in the distance, and the sun was bright overhead. On our way to the winery we drove through a leafy green tunnel of trees. I was in awe.

The main building in the vineyard was decorated for Christmas with a huge, festive bow on the roof. We parked and went inside where Eddie paid for our tastings. At the tasting counter, we were met by a woman who told us about all the wines. I was amazed by how many tastings we were offered and told Eddie as much. He agreed while simultaneously throwing back the first glass.

"Thirsty?" I joked.

He nodded. "This is delicious, I really like this one."

He was having a great time, but I could sense there was something on his mind. Figuring he'd tell me eventually, I waited until he was ready.

When we were done with our tastings, he asked if I would take a walk with him. I loved being outside and the winery was gorgeous. The mountain ranges in the background were so clear and beautiful they looked like a painting. Eddie grasped onto my hand as we walked, eventually leading me down a serene walkway bordered by trees. When we emerged in a small, lush grotto of vines and flowers, he pulled me close and kissed me.

Then he drew back and said, "You make me the happiest man on this planet. Forget planet, in the galaxy! Yeah, I said it!"

I started to giggle. "You make me even happier than that," I said, kissing him again.

Eddie told me how much he loved me and how much better his life was with me in it. He then mentioned that he'd asked my dad a very important question and received his blessing.

He reached into his pocket and pulled out a beautiful, sparkling, princess-cut diamond ring and dropped to one knee.

"Will you continue making me this happy by becoming my wife?"

I jumped into his arms. "Of course I'll marry you!"

Our engagement in California, December 27, 2009.

For a long time he held me close. It was a beautiful moment. Unforgettable. As we started walking back, Diana ran toward us, hugging me and squealing with joy. Eddie's mom and dad, Walter and Jeanine, sister Clare and his brother Tommy were all smiling and waiting for their turn to congratulate us.

Later, I found out that Diana had known all along. She'd even flown out to Texas to help Eddie pick out my ring.

Lying in bed that night, I asked Eddie, "Being that you're deploying at the end of next year, do you think we'll be able to have a wedding before then?"

"I think we can do it," he replied confidently.

I knew nothing about planning a wedding, but even I knew planning one in less than a year was going to be difficult. It didn't really bother me though. We'd figure it out.

*   *   *

Whenever I was stressed out or worried about the future, Eddie would remind me that he only had two more years in the Army, and that when he was done we'd have our whole lives ahead of us. He was my rock and I was his. There was nothing in the world we couldn't do as long as we did it together.

Eddie and I had discussed moving in together in the past, and revisiting that conversation, I never felt more sure about anything. Living together would not only make perfect sense but would also be a lot of fun. What better way to wake up every day than next to my best friend? We hated having to fly to see each other and really wanted the opportunity to be together all the time. The only thing holding me back was that I was attending graduate school at Long Island University in New York and I'd already signed up for classes for the coming semester. We decided that I would finish the semester, then move in with him in June until he deployed in October. I would have plenty of time to finish my master's degree while he was deployed.

Even though we had months until he left, the future stayed on our minds. It wasn't long before we decided that although we still wanted a wedding, we couldn't wait. We wanted to be married *now*. We kept our plans private from everyone but Diana, because we didn't want it to detract from the official celebration our friends and family wanted to share with us.

So, on January 15, 2010, Diana and I picked up Eddie from the airport and we drove straight to the City Clerk's Office in New City, New York. The ceremony was sweet and intimate, and the judge and staff very kind. It was a day I'll never forget. From then on, when we were in New York, Eddie was still my fiancé, but when I visited him in Louisiana, he was my husband.

The next few months kept me busy. I was working full time as well as going to classes and my internship after work. I was also planning a wedding, and Eddie and I were flying back and forth every other weekend. The flurry of activity helped the time fly, and finally we moved into our first apartment together. Even though there weren't a ton of things to do in Leesville, Louisiana, I was still elated to move. When it came to being with Eddie, I would have gone anywhere.

The more time I spent in Louisiana with Eddie, the more I learned about the military lifestyle. The military friends I made soon became an extended family and that connection helped me weather the trials of Army life. We all looked out for each other, supporting each other through times of necessary separation and eagerly celebrating homecomings.

The summer flew by, and on September 4 we had a beautiful evening wedding at a gorgeous venue in

New York. My bridesmaids in lavender dresses, groomsmen in black suits with matching lavender ties, led the way down the white carpeted aisle. Happy faces met mine as the double doors opened and I stepped into the chapel squeezing my dad's arm.

My nerves disappeared as I spotted Eddie across the room. Our smiles grew so wide that my cheeks hurt. Our family and friends shared our happiness as we exchanged our vows and danced the night away. We honeymooned on St. Lucia in the Caribbean.

The new Mr. and Mrs. Bolen

Siblings Clare, Franky, Andrea, Eddie, Diana, Tommy.

I had everything I wanted—peace, happiness, and of course, Eddie.

By the time we returned home to Louisiana, my anxiety resurfaced. Eddie was scheduled to deploy at the end of October to complete his final overseas assignment. This was the final stretch. After, he would return from deployment and only have a few months left in the Army. We planned on moving back to New York where Eddie would apply for the FDNY and finish school. As his deployment grew nearer, my sleep grew restless. I'd never known such fear in my life. This time, Eddie was going to Afghanistan.

Eddie would always tell me not to worry, that he would be fine. Knowing how scared I was, he always sugarcoated things for me when it came to deployments.

One night, we were sitting at the dinner table talking about the deployment.

"Are you scared to go?" I asked.

He looked at me and thought for a minute before responding. "Yeah. I'm not looking forward to it. But I'll be okay. The hardest part is being away from you."

I gave him a big kiss and hugged him. "Please promise me you're not going to try to be a hero. Do what you have to do, but please be careful. No crazy stuff." My eyes started tearing up.

Gently kissing my tears away, he said, "Don't worry baby, I'll be careful. After this is all over, we'll be together again and can go wherever we want."

I pulled him closer, desperate for his touch. "I don't know what I'd do without you."

We held each other for a long time, connecting and savoring our precious moments together.

*   *   *

Time again became my companion. Sometimes, slowing down, sometimes accelerating. It all depended on my emotions. But no matter what, it always moved forward, and the day we dreaded finally arrived. I secretly tucked a letter in his duffle bag before he loaded the car, and we drove to the post to say our final goodbyes.

Eddie did his best to keep the mood light, telling me how much he loved me and assuring me that everything would be fine. At the base, soldiers in his unit readied for departure, embracing their loved ones for as long as they could. When it was time for them to go, Eddie and I held each other tightly until the very last minute. He kissed every inch of my face.

"I'll call you as soon as I can. I love you always and forever."

"I love you too, baby. Always and forever."

At the last possible second, we let each other go.

The unit marched in unison, approaching the caravan of buses waiting at the end of the road. I couldn't take my eyes off Eddie. He turned his head and our eyes locked. He winked and gave me his signature, big smile. It was the same smile from the moment we first met, that smile that always greeted me at the airport and when I walked down the aisle. I smiled back at him, fighting the tears.

That was the last time I ever saw him.

Chapter Three

TRAGIC NEWS

At 3:08 a. m. on November 10, 2010, my eyes flew open. The room around me was pitch black. All I could see was the red light from the digital display coming from my alarm clock. I panicked and reached for my phone, hoping I hadn't missed a call from Eddie. I didn't have any messages but I couldn't ignore the constant ache I felt from our separation. I was anxious to hear from him. Eventually, I fell back into a restless sleep consumed by negative thoughts.

In the morning, I woke up feeling out-of-sorts. I rationalized that my uneasiness stemmed from attending a wake for my neighbor's twenty-year-old son the night before. Attending services for one so young never feels right and stays with you for days. Rolling out of bed, I immediately checked my email and Facebook account, but didn't have any messages from Eddie.

What I did find was a Facebook status from a military wife offering prayers for our men because our soldiers were being killed. The words made me sick to my stomach. I quickly asked her what had happened and who was involved. She responded that she hadn't meant anyone in particular, just in general. But my senses were up and I knew right away that something was wrong. That very morning, the same woman commented on one of my wedding photos.

I couldn't shake my anxiety. I called one of my closest friends at Fort Polk, Meghann, and told her what was going on. Meghann was a fellow military wife whose husband was stationed with Eddie in Afghanistan. I trusted her to tell me the truth. She never had a problem speaking her mind, which was one of the things I loved most about her. Talking to her was comforting. She told me not to worry and that if anything happened, I would be the first to know. Figuring that no news was good news, I tried to stop worrying. Of course, that's easier said than done. I kept my phone glued to my hip, impatiently waiting for Eddie to call.

The last time I spoke to him was Monday night, two days prior. I loved seeing that five-digit number on my phone or the crazy string of nineteen numbers denoting a call from another country. We joked about the shower he took a couple of days before, his first since he arrived. It consisted of fifteen seconds of cold water spurting from a bag he had to hold above his head.

We also chatted about my seven-month-old nephew, whose picture I received prior to Eddie's deployment. Despite the cuteness of Franky sitting in a green bucket, he was sporting a Red Sox onesie. As a big Yankees fan, that definitely got under my skin. When I told Eddie, his response was the same as mine, "No way! Not Franky. I'll have to talk to him about that." The two of us had a friendly, ongoing battle with my brother about which sports teams Franky should be supporting.

The day before our phone call, however, I looked more closely at the picture and realized that not only was Franky not wearing a Red Sox onesie, he was wearing the "Daddy's All-Star" onesie I gave him. I immediately started laughing and couldn't wait to tell Eddie. When he called, I blurted out, "Wait until you hear this!" At my news, Eddie laughed so hard. I always loved his laugh. It came from deep within his belly, and I could tell he was smiling just from the tone.

We spoke for about twenty minutes. I filled him in on what was going on in New York, and he told me a little bit about Afghanistan. He was sugarcoating everything, of course, so I wouldn't worry. Eventually, Eddie told me other soldiers were waiting for the phones and his time was up. We said, "I love you" about fifty times, trying to stay on the line for as long as we could. When we hung up, missing him created a huge knot of pain in my stomach. I didn't know it then, but that was the last time I ever spoke to my husband.

*   *   *

November 10, two days after our phone call, also marked my first day at my internship working with developmentally disabled adults. As I sat through the lectures that morning, I ceaselessly checked my phone every chance I got.

The instructor, Dante, was a really friendly guy in his mid-thirties. He had a shaved head, goatee, and a big smile that lit up his face. I enjoyed talking to him because he had an outgoing demeanor and reminded me of Eddie. During our break we were chatting about how dependent people are on their phones. I decided not to share why I was so attached to mine that day. I didn't want to get into that discussion and make myself even more nervous than I already was. Instead, I focused on the positives. Orientation was going well and I was excited to tell Eddie about it.

During our lunch break, I planned on going to the post office to mail Eddie a package. On my way, I received a call from my mom. She asked what I was doing and I told her I would be home soon. Her voice was short and unsteady. She told me not to go to the post office and to come straight home. A knot of dread instantly crystallized in my stomach. I asked her what was going on and once again, she told me to just come home. I could tell how hard it was for her to try to keep a calm voice. I hung up but immediately called her back, begging, "Please, Mom, what's going on?" In a shaky voice, she said, "Just please come home."

That five-minute drive felt like an eternity. I automatically thought the worst and felt lightheaded. My hands shook on the steering wheel.

There better not be an unknown car at my house!

When I pulled up to the house, I saw an unfamiliar blue Toyota Corolla parked in the driveway. My heart sank as my breaths came short and quick. Trembling all over, I raced inside.

As I opened the door to the kitchen, I saw my mom standing next to two soldiers in their Class A uniforms. I immediately slammed the door and stepped outside. Nausea gripped me. Tears poured from my eyes. It was difficult to breathe. My mom ran outside after me and hugged me as we cried together. I could barely stand. My legs were weak and my heart was pounding harder than before. Finally, with my mom at my side, I gathered the strength to walk back in the house. As I stared at the men, all I could think was *Please tell me he's hurt. Whatever it is, I'll be on the next flight out to Germany to be with him. We can get through this. Just tell me he's only hurt.*

I was in a fog. I could see the soldiers' mouths moving but could barely hear their words. I was suspended and numb, waiting to hear one of two words: either injured or killed. My heart pounded painfully to life as one of the soldiers informed me he was from West Point and that the other man was a chaplain. I couldn't grasp whatever else was said. All I cared about was hearing what state Eddie was in. Then, the soldier told me about an IED exploding and said the words that will haunt me for the rest of my life.

"Sgt. Bolen was killed in the explosion."

It couldn't be. I hadn't heard them right. No, they had the wrong guy. There was no way that my Eddie was gone. No way that this incredible person who was always so full of love and life had been taken from this world.

As the truth slowly began to sink in, all of my happiness was sucked out of me as fast as that IED took my husband's life. I may not remember word-for-word what was said that horrible day, but I will never forget the two men who told me the worst news of my life. The look in their sunken, grief-stricken eyes and how terrified they were to tell me that my greatest fear had been realized. The fear most military families hope never to face just became my reality.

My shell of numbness was already cracking under the force of the excruciating pain in my heart. I didn't know what to do next. The thought came to me that I had friends who were still over there. I asked if there were any other casualties. They informed me that one other soldier was injured but no one else was killed. Opposing emotions of relief and anger warred inside me. *How could the love of my life have been taken from this earth? Could this have been prevented? He'd just arrived. It hadn't even been two weeks!*

So many thoughts and questions tumbled through my head, but I couldn't speak. I was handed a card with my casualty officer's name and number, and was told that he would be coming by within the next few days. As the men left, anger again swept through me. They had to be wrong. How could this happen to my Eddie?

I went to my room and lay for a while on my bed, crying and thinking about what I needed to do next. I decided I had to call Carson, Eddie's best man at our wedding. My fingers shook as I tried to pull his name up on my contact list. I stared at the phone for a few minutes before I was finally able to push the call button.

After a few rings, his chipper voice greeted me. "'Ello gov'na!"

Nearly choking on my tears, I blurted, "Carson!"

"Dre? What's wrong?"

I should have asked where he was, if he was driving, if he was alone. But I couldn't think straight. I had to tell him.

"Eddie was killed in Afghanistan!" I cried.

Saying the words aloud triggered a wave of anguish inside me, Carson's answering screams compounded my pain.

"NO! NO! NO! NOT EDDIE! NO!"

For five minutes, I sat on the other end of the phone sobbing as I told him over and over again that it was true. That was the hardest phone call I ever had to make, not only because I had to deliver the awful news, but because I needed to ask him to do me a really difficult favor.

Carson was in the Navy and stationed in San Diego, only forty-five minutes from the Bolens. He was also very close with the family. I felt horrible for asking something of him that would no doubt be painful, but I had to.

"They had to make sure I was the first to get the news," I told him. "Now they'll send someone to tell his parents. There's no way his mom can hear the news from a stranger, and I can't do it over the phone. I know this is so hard, but I need you to tell the Bolens."

My heart broke even further for his willing sacrifice. I couldn't imagine having to give Eddie's parents the news myself, but even more importantly, there was no way I could do it over the phone. I made sure Carson had someone to drive him and told him I would call their other best friend, Finny, before we said tearful goodbyes.

With trembling hands, I dialed Finny's number. "Hey Dre!" he answered in a cheerful voice.

I tried to compose myself but knew I wasn't doing a good job. I asked him if he was driving and told him he needed to pull over. I could hear the fear in his voice. I didn't say anything else until he was safely parked.

"Okay, I'm on the side of the road. What's up?"

His tone assured me that he was ready to hear what I had to say. He was braced for impact. I proceeded to blurt out as much as I could remember. He took the news a lot more calmly than Carson, but I could tell he was in shock. Thankfully, he was in the car with his girlfriend and she would get him back home safely.

As the details emerged, he kept asking about me and what he could do. Typical Finny—always the strong one. After we hung up, I thought to myself, *I can't keep making these phone calls.*

But there was one more I had to make, to Meghann. In light of our conversation that morning, I knew I had to tell her. I needed my friend's support. When she answered, I didn't ask where she was or what she was doing. I just exploded into tears and haltingly told her what happened. Between sobs, I cried, "They came to my house! The soldiers came! It was Eddie. Meg it was Eddie!" Meghann cried with me, devastated because she knew the fear every military wife shared. A fear that was now my reality.

About two hours later, my phone rang. It was Eddie's mom, Jeanine. I knew the call meant that Carson had delivered the news. I stared at her name on my Caller ID and tried to valiantly pull myself together. It was impossible. I could barely speak when I answered the phone, and managed only a whispered hello.

Jeanine was crying. "Please tell me it's not true," she begged. "It can't be true."

My face soaked with tears, but I managed to stammer out, "It's true, it's true, I can't believe it's true. The two soldiers came to my house."

We cried on the phone for a long time, sharing in our overwhelming misery. Before hanging up, I spoke with Eddie's younger brother, Tommy. He kept asking about me and if I was okay. He was so much like Eddie, always looking out for everyone else.

I asked Jeanine if she wanted me to tell Clare, Eddie's younger sister, but she said she'd do it. Clare was attending school in Albany at the time, about two hours from me. When she heard the news, her roommates piled in the car and drove her to my house. That only left my sister, Diana, who was in Buffalo. My mom called her for me, and when I got on the phone all I could say was, "You have to get home, I need you here, please come home." She flew home a few hours later.

The next thing I knew, friends and family started showing up at my house. My memory of that day is a shapeless blur of crying, hugging, drinking, and even some people laughing. I do remember knocking back shots like a champ. Eddie would have laughed at the sight and reminded me, "You're not that softball player in college anymore." I couldn't eat, I drank like a fish, but was miraculously spared a hangover. That, I was sure, was Eddie's doing. He knew I didn't need any more pain. That night, my parents gave their room to Clare, Diana, and me. We lay in bed holding each other and crying our eyes out. I had my two sisters on either side, sharing my pain. I don't think any of us got more than an hour of sleep.

Chapter Four

GASPING FOR AIR

Though I hadn't asked him to come, Finny woke up early the next morning and drove five hours to be with me. He knew we needed each other. His own heart was broken, but he showed up to support me and spent the day sharing my tears and trying to make me laugh.

Several reporters gathered outside my house. My dad called the newspaper that morning because he wanted Eddie to be recognized for his sacrifice. He figured they would print a small article describing the kind of man Eddie was and how he fought for our country. He certainly didn't expect reporters to come to the house and ask for interviews. None of us could believe the response. My dad spoke to a reporter and told him that we have a strong family and they were there for me. When they kept asking, he told them I didn't want to be interviewed.

I wanted Eddie to have the publicity he deserved and for the world to know about his strength of character and the sacrifice he made. I definitely did not want to be in the spotlight or have cameras in my face. I was a complete mess and knew I wouldn't be able to handle that kind of chaos. Thankfully, Finny came to my rescue. With a gift for eloquence, along with an approachable personality, he took over speaking with the reporters. At my request, he told them to publicize that in lieu of flowers, our families would appreciate donations to the Wounded Warriors Foundation. Over the next few days, reporters showed up as well as a stream of delivery people. Edible arrangements, flowers and food all arrived on our doorstep. Finny made sure to go outside and greet them, each time someone pulled up to the house. He didn't want me to have to deal with any of it.

My house quickly filled up with people, food, and flowers. Family members came, as well as a parade of friends and neighbors. My phone rang constantly, and texts flooded my phone. Despite how overwhelming it all was, I couldn't turn off my phone until I knew that my friends in Afghanistan were okay. Finally, my phone rang displaying a call from the same crazy, unknown number that my husband used to call me from when he was deployed. This was the call I was waiting for, and also the one I feared the most.

My hands were shaking so hard I could barely answer the phone. It was the voices that I had been waiting to hear. I wanted to make sure that they were safe and unharmed, but I also needed them to tell me that it was all a big mistake and that it wasn't Eddie. My thoughts cycled rapidly from worry to hope and back again. *They got the wrong guy. Please tell me Eddie's okay.*

I spoke with Dan, Sean, and Jon, all good friends of ours. Their voices were thick and choked with pain. Eddie and I were extremely close with Sean in particular, whose wife, Melissa, was still living in Pennsylvania while he lived near us in Louisiana. Eddie and I looked out for him and had him over to our apartment often. I begged Sean to tell me it was all a mistake. He couldn't. He was there when Eddie was killed and his first words, "I'm so sorry, Dre," reopened the pain in my heart and destroyed any shred of hope I had left. I experienced the horrible news all over again. I knew how difficult it was for them to call me, as the pain in their own hearts was clear. They assured me that they were okay. I was relieved to hear it, and wished they could be with me so I could wrap my arms around them. After that final phone call, I turned off my phone. I wanted nothing to do with it anymore. The only other call I wanted was one I would never receive again.

Sitting all around me at the kitchen table were people I loved, but I felt totally alone. I couldn't speak or hear what anyone else was saying. Grief surrounded me, totally blocking me off from the world. Everyone was blurry and indistinct. Sounds became muffled. I felt like I was stuck in the center of a tornado of misery while the world revolved without me.

Friends came and left, some crying with pain in their eyes. Others came with smiles, trying to be strong and supportive. All the while, I sat frozen, unable to escape the chaos destroying everything around me. Life as I knew it was over. My love and happiness had shattered. As lost as I was, though, I was still grateful for the gift of having loved ones surrounding me. Alcohol continued to flow, shot after shot appearing before me. Each person made a different toast to the beautiful life of Eddie Bolen.

Finally, I reached a point that night when I could no longer stand being around people. The nonstop, well-intentioned affection was beginning to suffocate me. I snuck away to my room and lay on my bed facing the wall. It was dark, but I could still see the pictures of my husband everywhere. I cried and cried and cried. Just when I thought I was too tired to cry anymore, I cried even harder.

Eventually, I heard someone come into the room, felt arms around me, and heard the soft words, "Hey Dre, I love you." It was Finny. I wasn't surprised. Of course he would come to check on me. At that moment, I needed him more than he would ever know. He kept his arms around me and let me cry while trying to hold me together as I fell apart. I felt better with him there. He gave me a safe space to weep and rant, and rocked me until I finally fell asleep. Although I didn't sleep for long, Finny's presence allowed me to calm down enough to drift off for a little while.

*　　*　　*

The following morning, I noticed Diana staring out the kitchen window. Joining her, I saw that her attention was on a small black car parked just around the corner from our house. As we watched, a tall man with an athletic build stepped out. He appeared to be in his thirties and wore a newly pressed immaculate, Class A uniform. His whole demeanor embodied honor and respect. It would have been presentable to Eddie's high standards. My husband was very particular about maintaining a perfectly organized uniform. His normal civilian clothes, on the other hand, were a completely different story. Those shirts rarely came into contact with an iron.

Diana and I watched the unknown man gather his things and glance at his reflection in the car window, making sure his uniform was neat and everything was in its proper place. Clearly he needed a moment to collect his thoughts before approaching the house. When he finally knocked on the door and my parents opened it, he was calm and very professional.

"Hello, I'm Major Johnston, Mrs. Bolen's casualty officer. I'm so sorry for your loss. I'm here to help her throughout this process."

Standing in the dining room, I listened to my parents greet the major. Then my sister asked in a teasing tone, "Why did you park around the corner?"

"You were watching me?" he asked, a little nervous and surprised.

Diana laughed, trying to lighten the mood and make the major feel a little more comfortable if that was at all possible.

We all sat at the kitchen table and the major began to outline what steps I needed to take. There was so much to go over regarding the funeral, Eddie's belongings in Afghanistan, and our belongings that were still in Louisiana. The paperwork seemed endless. I grasped maybe a quarter of what the major was saying, but my mind wandered to memories of Eddie and me sitting at the table prior to his deployment, discussing all the documents that needed to be completed before he left.

Eddie wanted to talk through everything with me, even though his looming deployment was an emotional topic. I'd been angry that he was required to fill out papers like a will, power of attorney, where he wanted to be buried, and who would make decisions about the funeral. Distraught, I told him how horrible it all was and that I didn't want to think about it.

"Those men in uniform better not come to my house and deliver me that horrible news. I'll be at the airport waiting for you, just like I was when you came back from Iraq."

He gave me a loving look. "Aw, sweetheart, don't worry. This is just something that we have to do. I'll be fine." He wrapped his arms around me and kissed me. "I love you so much baby. You're an amazing, strong woman and I'm so lucky to have you standing by me and supporting me. After this deployment, we can finally move back to New York and start the rest of our lives together."

His tone was soft yet strong, and I took comfort in his smile. "You better not let anything happen to you," I insisted. "I don't know what I would do without you."

His smile widened. "Pshh, you think I'd ever leave you? You're crazy. You're stuck with me baby." He batted his puppy-dog eyes. "I love you so much my beautiful wife."

"I love you too, Eddie. Always and forever."

I played that conversation over and over in my head until I reverted back to reality when I heard my mom call my name. The major passed me a pen and patiently explained each of the papers I needed to fill out and sign. Seeing how much I was struggling, he spoke clearly and slowly for me to follow along. He then explained the dignified transfer of remains that would occur at Dover Air Force Base in Delaware. He outlined the details of the somber ritual. Upon the aircraft's landing, a team of military personnel would transfer the casket to the vehicle that would then travel to the port mortuary. There, I would be able to welcome Eddie home.

Later that day, after listening to several voicemail messages, I came across a number I didn't know. The voicemail was from Sgt. Shane Adams, stationed at Fort Polk in Louisiana, who was assigned to escort Eddie to Dover. His heavy Southern accent triggered a memory and I recalled meeting him briefly at one of the company softball games. I decided to call him back. He was warm and caring, instantly putting me at ease. I could tell how honored he was to be able to do this for Eddie.

*   *   *

On the night of November 12th, two days after the news, Major Johnston came to pick up Clare, Diana, and me. He drove us to Dover in a van that was issued to him from West Point. It was an uneventful three-hour ride but seemed to take forever because of our collective mental and emotional exhaustion. I don't remember if Diana and Clare fell asleep, but my mind and heart didn't allow me to rest.

We arrived at the hotel around one in the morning. The outside air felt like ice against my skin. The lobby was quiet, but the hotel staff knew why we were there and greeted us warmly. We were brought to a small conference room to discuss how the transfer worked and what to expect. A table in the room held snacks and drinks, along with handmade scarves for us. I hadn't eaten all day but couldn't even bring myself to look at the food. Diana was starving and took advantage of the kindness, heating a can of soup in a nearby microwave. It was one of those soups you could drink right from the container. Watching her wrestle with the wrapper to try to figure it out was a small but welcome entertainment.

I was sitting in a chair staring at the wall when I realized that Clare was gently playing with my hair. I didn't know how much I craved comfort until that moment. I wrapped my arms around her and squeezed, fighting to keep myself together for her. I was the older sister, I felt like I should be the strong one, but nothing could be further from the truth. Without Diana and Clare's support, I would have fallen apart.

The next two hours passed with excruciating slowness. Time was once again my enemy. I gave consent to allow media coverage for the dignified transfer and agreed with the caveat that the reporters would stay away from me. We waited another two hours for the Bolens to arrive, as military personnel had provided them with a flight from California. Conversation in the room was sparse, silence stretching unbroken for long periods. Clare and Diana periodically paced around the room while I sat in my chair numbly and stared at a wall.

Finally, around three o'clock in the morning, we greeted Eddie's parents and brother in the lobby. I put on a brave face, but as soon as I saw them the tears came pouring down. Walter was the first to greet me, wrapping me in his arms and murmuring words of comfort and sorrow. It was particularly hard to see him, as Eddie looked so much like his father. My embraces with Jeanine and Tommy were a mix of pain and comfort. We were all reunited and now waiting on just one more person—Eddie.

The military representatives explained once more what would happen, though the knowledge didn't dent anyone's anxiety. Tommy, Diana, and I stayed in the conference room. It was such a relief to be around Tommy. Although he's younger, his demeanor and heart evoked fond memories of Eddie. Tommy did whatever he could to make me smile during that tense time, just as Eddie would have done.

We shared memories of Eddie, joking that he'd love getting all this attention. We reminisced about our favorite memories of his personality quirks, especially how animated and excited he'd get over the smallest of things. That conversation turned into a lengthy discussion of scenarios in which we speculated on WWED, or What Would Eddie Do? I was able to laugh for the first time since his death even though it was short-lived.

Two hours later we were informed of the aircraft's imminent arrival and a whirlwind of anxiety and misery washed over me, intermixed with relief that Eddie was finally coming home. We were escorted to a large bus that took us to the runway. I spent the short trip in the backseat with Walter, his arm wrapped tightly around me. When we arrived we were escorted to a roped-off area to wait.

Not until a blanket surrounded my shoulders did I realize my whole body was trembling. It wasn't the cold affecting me but the soberness of the moment. I stood and waited with Tommy on my left and Diana on my right. The rest of the Bolens lined up beside Diana.

Time contracted and relaxed as my heart raced frantically. *It's a mistake. They got the wrong guy. Eddie's still alive. This nightmare will be over soon.* But the wish my heart longed for was denied.

My breathing quickened as the back latch of the C-17 Globemaster opened and the landing ramp descended. The plane's huge interior seemed hollow, occupied by only a few military personnel. Then, as the landing hit the ground, I saw the image that will never escape my memory. The beautiful colors of the American flag so delicately draped over the casket. The casket my husband was in. It looked so small in the cavernous space. I felt a jumble of emotions. I wanted so desperately to leap across the tarmac to Eddie's coffin and drape my arms over it.

My eyes burned as tears flowed anew. Six men in pristine uniforms walked to the casket and saluted Eddie. They clasped the handles and slowly marched down the ramp in unison to the waiting vehicle in a dignified and respectful manner. Reality came crashing down on my shoulders and my heart broke to pieces. Eddie was in that casket. My husband was home, but this was nothing like how I'd imagined it.

My tears came faster and harder. My knees weakened. I didn't realize I was slowly going down until Tommy wrapped his arm around me. He stood strong and brave, supporting my weight and my grief as we watched my husband being carried toward the transport vehicle. The soldiers delicately loaded the casket into the back, saluting a final time, before closing the doors and marching away. The vehicle slowly drove toward the exit. The entire transfer was beautiful, dignified, and respectful, but the pain of those moments scarred my mind and heart forever.

As the vehicle disappeared and the taillights diminished, a wondrous change occurred above us. Darkness was swept away by light, dawn painting the sky with the most beautiful reds and oranges I had ever seen. It felt like the sunrise itself was welcoming Eddie home.

"Welcome home, my love," I whispered.

AP Photo/Jose Luis Magana

The dignified transfer at Dover, November 2010

Chapter Five

SAYING GOODBYE

The next few days consisted of visits from family and friends, as we toasted to Eddie and laughed and cried in memory of a wonderful man. The Bolens drove up to Chittenango, New York, to be with their friends and family while we stayed in Rockland for a couple more days, waiting to find out when we could have the services. It takes a long time for the coroner to release a body for burial in the military.

I needed to pack a bag in preparation to travel to Chittenango for the services, but the thought of picking out something to wear to my husband's funeral overwhelmed me. When I tried, I ended up just staring blankly into my closet. Such moments inevitably ended with me slamming the closet door and deciding to do it later.

The days blurred together, but one moment shines bright in my memory. A few friends were keeping me company when my phone rang. It was my mother-in-law, Jeanine.

"Andrea, you won't believe this," she stammered.

"What's going on?" I asked.

"I just spoke to the funeral director. He said the church isn't big enough to fit all the people they anticipate coming. Eddie's high school offered to close the school for the day and hold the services in the gymnasium."

It took me a moment to digest her words.

"Andrea?"

I found my voice. "Yes, I'm here. I can't believe it. How many people are they expecting?"

"He's saying hundreds."

I couldn't believe his school would do that, but at the same time it felt so perfect. For Eddie, bigger was always better, and this was huge. He spoke often about his high school days, and I knew how honored he would have been about this. I was just glad he'd be getting the recognition he deserved.

Jeanine and I discussed more details, deciding I would come up the following day to help with the arrangements. After I hung up, I realized everyone was staring at me because they could see the look of shock on my face.

Eddie would love knowing his school was closing to honor him and I smiled at the thought. I could easily imagine the smug look on his face and his remark, "Guess who closed all the schools in the district? This guy!" I closed my eyes, picturing his smile as we danced around in celebration. For that brief moment, I felt him with me.

*   *   *

They were finally able to give us the date of the services. The wake would be on Friday and the funeral on Saturday—ten days after I received the news. It was hard, knowing Eddie was still at the mortuary in Dover. I wanted so badly to be with him. I floated between aggravation that everything was taking so long, and sorrow knowing that in a few days it would all be over and I would be burying my husband. It was surreal, and a part of me was still in denial.

To this very day, a part of me can't quite believe he's really gone.

We left for Syracuse the next day. It was another long and quiet car ride. I went with my family and the Bolens to the floral shop and the funeral home to make arrangements. As we walked through the doors of the floral shop, I could feel eyes on us, yet I couldn't really say much. The thought of picking out flowers for my husband's funeral made me nauseous. They gave us a booklet to look through and all I could do was stare at the pages. My mind was elsewhere.

My mom pointed out a beautiful arrangement of red roses forming a heart. The red was as deep as blood and I thought, *how appropriate*. I was in so much pain that I felt as if my heart was literally bleeding. The roses were gorgeous, but it was difficult to wrap my head around the thought of where they would be going. That was the beautiful arrangement I decided on, with a sash that said "Beloved Husband."

Next stop was the funeral parlor. A kind man named Mr. Zimmer approached us and gave his condolences. He was professionally dressed in a neat black suit and tie. His son and Eddie had played sports and gone to high school together. As Mr. Zimmer and the Bolens went through the details, I drifted back into my mind, entertaining the fantasy that at any moment, Eddie would call and tell me that there had been a mistake and he was fine. I even felt sorry for the family who would get the bad news once the real identity of the soldier was confirmed. I decided no matter where that soldier was from, I would go to the services to pay my respects.

"Andrea?" whispered my mom. I snapped back to the present, the sting erupting in my heart at the shift from fantasy to reality.

Eddie was gone.

The mood that evening was bittersweet. We spent it at the family home of one of Eddie's best friends, Carson Lindsey. The Lindseys had known Eddie since his childhood and were dear friends of the Bolens. Eddie's friends filled the house. Most I knew and some I hadn't met yet. We had an informal celebration of Eddie's life. Everyone shared an anecdote or funny story about Eddie. I couldn't help but feel a sense of comfort being with everyone, especially since Eddie would have been so happy that we were all together. We all felt the love we had for one another, as well as the deep pain of losing such a special person.

Carson's flight home was scheduled to arrive the next day, but heavy fog kept delaying it. Even though he was having such a hard time, he was able to joke on the phone that the weather was probably Eddie messing with him. He finally arrived home late that evening. Desperate to see him, I drove with his father and brother to pick him up from the airport. Our reunion was tearful and comforting all at once. We held each other tightly, drawing from each other the strength we'd need in the coming days.

The next day we spent time creating picture boards to hang at the funeral. Each photo and memory was like a sharp knife entering my open wounds. I found comfort in being around loved ones and it was fun to see Clare and Carson's board filled with photos of a much younger Eddie. But I still couldn't help the pain when I saw his smiling face, knowing he was gone.

The following day we arrived at the funeral home where two limos and a hearse were waiting. After a twenty-five minute drive, we arrived at Hancock Field, the Air National Guard Base of the Syracuse airport. Eddie was returning to his beloved hometown. While we were driving, I noticed hundreds of American flags forming a trail along the side of the road. I figured they were from Veteran's Day, a week before. As we exited the car I noticed two parallel lines of American flags creating a runway. Lined up were at least fifty men on motorcycles wearing jackets that said Patriot Guard Riders. Chills rolled over me as I recalled Eddie telling me a story about them. They come together and ride during military funerals to protect the grieving family from harassment against protesters from the Westboro Baptist church. The protesters are a small congregation of intolerant Christian fanatics from the Westboro Baptist Church who claim military deaths are God's punishment for American tolerance of LGBTQ people. They use military funerals to attract attention to their evil-mindedness. The Patriot Guard Riders shield the protesters from the service by lining in formation. Some hold big flags and others will rev their motorcycle engines to drain out their chants. The protestors are anti-gay not anti-war. Gay, straight, bisexual, black, white, doesn't matter to me. But what I still can't wrap my head around is that is has nothing to do with the military.

When he told me this, I felt sick at the notion that there were people in this world heartless enough to show such hurtful disrespect to the family of a fallen soldier.

Now that I was a part of that family, I knew I would go berserk if I saw any protesters at Eddie's services. But the comfort of knowing that we'd be protected, that so many people would be around me, lifted that weight from my shoulders. The Patriot Guard Riders were a Godsend. Their pride and respect for the fallen was a voluntary gift, welcomed and appreciated and immeasurably touching.

Again, all we could do was wait. We stood outside anxiously waiting for Eddie to arrive. As I noticed the jet in the distance, I realized I was holding my breath. I reflected back on all the times I waited for him at the airport. Seeing him walk from the terminal with that big, beautiful smile as he picked me up and swung me around. I wiped away the tears rolling down my face. Today, there were no smiles, no laughter, and my feet would stay firmly planted on the ground.

As the jet landed, his casket, draped in the American flag, was placed on the lift and then lowered to the ground. The ceremonial guards carried him to the hearse. After they closed the door I saw Sgt. Shane Adams approach me with a big hug. "Andrea, I'm so sorry for your loss. Eddie was a really great guy and soldier."

"Thank you for your support and for helping bring him home," I stammered. I knew it wasn't easy for him emotionally. He told me he would stay with Eddie the whole time when we were in Dover and escort him back home.

"It's an honor ma'am."

I looked to my right and instantly felt a sense of relief when I saw Eddie's former roommate, Sgt. Cary Davis, approaching me. I was so happy to see him and wrapped my arms around him for a comforting embrace. We'd spoken before he arrived but now there was nothing to say. I just knew I needed him there as much as he needed to be there. Once Eddie was secure in the hearse, we piled into the limos in complete silence. I didn't realize what was going to happen next. I'm sure Major Johnston told me several times but I was in such a fog that it was difficult to be mentally present. There was so much to take in and an immense amount of pain to really wrap my head around the reality of what was happening.

I could hear the motorcycle engines rev as half of the Patriot Guard Riders held the lead while the rest followed behind us. It felt like a protective, patriotic shield. Davis, dressed in his Class A's, sat to my right and stared out the window. As we drove out of the airport and into town, I again noticed the flags lining the streets. When our journey took us down unfamiliar streets, I wondered if the driver was taking a longer route then necessary. Then I realized what was happening.

Hundreds of people lined the sides of the roads waiting for us to pass. Some had flags, while others had signs. I looked in awe at the beautiful people who dropped everything to pay their respects to Eddie.

Men and women of all ages saluted as we went by, while little children waved their flags. The windows of some houses displayed painted messages, among them "Welcome Home, Sgt. Bolen," and "Thank You for Your Sacrifice SGT Bolen." It was the most overwhelming yet astounding display of human compassion I had ever witnessed.

The crowds continued, thickening as we progressed. Though it had started drizzling, no one moved. They suffered the cold to pay their respects. Seeing the outpouring of love from the town, I understood why Eddie was so proud to be from Chittenango. I wept at the incredible turnout for my husband and for the love so clearly visible around me. Our ride ended at the funeral home where Eddie was delicately held in preparation for the services.

Photo: Stephen D. Cannerelli, The Post-Standard

The funeral procession passed through the town of Chittenango. Hundreds in the community came out to pay their respects. The fire department hung a large American flag overhead.

That night, we went to the funeral home to visit Eddie. Due to the impact of the explosion, a closed casket was necessary. Not being able to see his beautiful face left a hole inside me that would never close. I yearned to touch him, to kiss him, but everyone assured me that it was better to not have that image of Eddie and to remember him the way that he was.

We were allowed to pass along personal items and letters that would be placed in the casket with him prior to burial. I had many things I wanted to leave him, and I might have gone a little overboard. I brought the last Harry Potter book, a golf club, his Vibram FiveFingers shoes that he loved, and a letter that I had written to him. The most important item, however, was the extra wedding band I gave him to wear in Afghanistan, engraved with the words *always and forever*. Others brought letters and other small objects that held sentimental value to them.

Clutching my bag of items, I approached Major Johnston, who had agreed to personally place its contents with Eddie. As I started walking, however, time slowed, stopped, and sped backward. I wasn't in the funeral home anymore. Looking around in awe, I was back in the apartment Eddie and I once shared. Our pictures still hung on the walls. The afghan blanket my mom made us was draped over our couch. The blinds were open, sunlight streaming in, and music drifted from my computer.

Any minute, Eddie would be home. I couldn't wait to give him the present I'd bought on a recent trip to New York. Surprising him with gifts was always exciting. He always had the best reaction—no matter how big or how small the gift was.

I heard the front door open, and seconds later my husband walked into the kitchen with a huge smile. After giving me a hug and a kiss hello, he walked into the other room to put down his bag. I followed him, with my hands behind my back, concealing the small box I held.

When I told him I got him something, his eyes lit up. Giddy with excitement, he tried to look behind my back. I teased him a while, darting back to avoid his hands, when he grabbed for the present I finally handed him the box. I could tell from his expression that he had no idea what it was.

When he cracked open the lid, his reaction surpassed my expectations. He was ecstatic, and when he saw the engraving on the ring his eyes became glassy. I told him that I commissioned the ring, so he could leave his original band safe at home with me while he was deployed. He immediately put it on, holding his hand up to the light like he was showing the ring off to a class during Show and Tell. Then he picked me up, dancing and swinging me around our living room. I couldn't stop laughing. I could have given him a coffee mug and he would have been just as excited.

But it was a dream, and as the vision crumbled around me, I was cruelly dumped back in the present. Major Johnston gently reached for the bag in my hands and asked if I was feeling okay. I wanted to scream out loud at the loss of the memory. I wanted to take time by the throat and demand I be returned to the past. Instead, I looked around at my world— the real one. I was in a dark funeral home standing next to my husband's casket. Nearby, people gathered in small groups consoling each other. Others spoke softly, and still more stared at me with concern. My heart started racing. I couldn't speak. All I could do was nod my head and hand him the bag.

I had never been to a military funeral before and didn't know what to expect. On the morning of the wake we were greeted by Mr. Zimmer and the funeral staff. While waiting outside I noticed that one of the Patriot Guards had come forward and was talking to my dad. With shock, I recognized him as my childhood friend and neighbor, Kyle. He had ridden three and a half hours on his motorcycle with his girlfriend in the freezing cold to be a part of the procession escorting the hearse to the school. My eyes began to tear. Those were my first tears of the day, though far from my last.

Soon, two limousines, a hearse, and a small van arrived outside the funeral home. Six soldiers wearing white gloves exited the van and straightened their uniforms. They looked so young and nervous. I remembered another story from Eddie about a funeral he had to work at a couple years prior. It was for a retired veteran who lived a full life. Eddie had been a little nervous, but also felt very honored to help pay his respects to a man he didn't know, yet greatly appreciated his service. Mr. Zimmer explained the transfer as we watched the casket being loaded into the hearse. It took every ounce of willpower I possessed to not throw myself at the casket. I could overhear a conversation going on with Finny and a police officer. He was explaining to Finny about the protesters obtaining a permit. My body tensed as I thought about lashing out at the cruel individuals who would have the audacity to come near my husband's funeral. The Patriot Guard rider close by could see the rage on my face and tried to reassure me. "Don't worry ma'am, this is why we're here. They won't come near this funeral!" I felt my body slightly relax. I was still furious but relieved to have these incredible, patriotic men present.

The Patriot Guard Riders rode at the front and the back of our procession, guiding us all the way to the school. As we neared our destination, more tears flowed when I saw the two fire trucks parked at the entrance. They were lined up with their buckets extended, and strung between them was a huge American flag in tribute. I whispered to Eddie, "Even the firemen came for you." Closing my eyes, I could see the joy on Eddie's face.

As we entered the school, we saw Patriot Guard Riders lining the hallway. Others stood in formation at the back of the gym, an American flag displayed reverently in their hands. Their love and respect created a shelter within, and I felt safe to both grieve and truly celebrate the life of my husband. I will forever be in their debt.

Rows of chairs covered the large floor of the gym. The bleachers were pulled out to accommodate the vast number of people they were anticipating. Eddie's casket was placed at the back of the gym draped with a bold, beautiful American flag. The picture boards we had made lined the sides of the gym leading to the casket. Next to it a table showcased the medals Eddie had been awarded, as well as a television showing the dignified transfer at Dover Air Force Base. I could barely look at the footage. My memory was painful enough.

As the crowd thickened, I saw many people I knew, some of whom had traveled great distances to be there. People I hadn't seen in years had traveled to offer their condolences. There were also many faces I'd never met, strangers as well as some I knew only by name. One young man in particular left a lasting impression. When he approached me, his eyes were red and swollen, and he had a difficult time looking at me.

"Ma'am, I'm so sorry for your loss. My name is Matt and I'm a Marine." His hand shook as he presented me with his own medals. "Your husband is a hero and I would be honored if you accepted my medals as a tribute to him."

I was floored and extremely touched. Although I felt conflicted taking his medals, I knew it was the right thing to do. I gave him a hug, thanking him for his offering and his service. Holding the medals to my chest, I then watched him stand before Eddie's casket. With tears in his eyes, he saluted my husband.

In that simple gesture, I saw the depthless camaraderie between soldiers, and the respect and pride possessed by military personnel for their country and each other.

I shook hundreds of hands and received hundreds of hugs from strangers and friends alike. After two hours, physical and emotional exhaustion took hold of me. I couldn't stand up by the casket anymore greeting everyone. Escaping to the bleachers, I joined my friends and my fellow military wives. My head was spinning and my body hummed. I wanted the relief of darkness and sleep, but my heart kept me there. This was for Eddie. As long as there were people who wanted to speak with me, to share a small part of my grief, I would stay. The day seemed to last forever.

*   *   *

Explosions and gunfire rock the desert around me. Through a veil of heavy smoke and dust, I see him. Eddie. I try to run toward him, but my legs feel unnaturally heavy, like I'm stuck in thick mud instead of standing on hard ground. With every ounce of strength I possess, I fight the force holding me back from my husband. Little by little, step by step, I close the distance between us.

Eddie smiles and opens his arms. I collapse against him, sobbing. His love radiates through me as he kisses my forehead.

"Eddie, are you okay? Did it hurt? Did you suffer?"

He lifts my chin so I can see his soft smile. "Don't worry about me, my love. I'm fine. I didn't feel a thing."

My eyes snapped open to a dark room. The sound of my rapid breathing filled my ears as I looked at the bedside clock. Two-thirty in the morning. That wasn't the first time I dreamt about Eddie, but this one was especially vivid. I felt his arms, saw his smile, and heard his voice.

Since his death I'd struggled with thoughts of what he felt at the end and if he'd been in pain. The thought of him suffering tore me apart. This dream was a gift—necessary, but painful. It comforted me even as it reopened the wound in my heart. I didn't fall back asleep after that, but lay in bed crying. When I was too tired to cry anymore, I stared at the dark wall, missing my husband with every fiber of my being.

When it was time to get up and prepare for the funeral, I walked dragging my joyless body to the bathroom to take a shower. Zombie-like, heavy and lifeless, I took off my clothes and stepped into the shower letting hot water pour over my head. I couldn't move. All I could do was cry. Eventually I mustered enough energy to finish showering, though every forward movement reminded me of that dream.

I was stuck in quicksand, but this time, no amount of effort would bring me back to Eddie. When I got out, I looked at myself in the mirror and didn't recognize the woman looking back at me. I'd lost weight and dark circles ringed my joyless eyes. This woman had lost her heart. This woman was me.

Chapter Six

A FINAL SALUTE

I didn't really care about my appearance, but I did want to look nice for Eddie. I blow-dried my hair and managed to put on a little mascara. Despite having worn them before, the black dress and tights chaffed my sensitive skin. Even my grey boots, soft and worn, felt restrictive. Nothing was right about this day. I slipped a black wrap around my shoulders and put on the beautiful ruby earrings Eddie had bought me in Iraq. I already wore his dog tags. He gave them to me when we started dating and I wore them often under my clothes. It provided a sense of comfort and felt like he was with me. I hadn't taken them off since I received the horrific news. I needed him close to me more then ever.

Standing before my full-length mirror, I wondered if this is how a widow was supposed to dress. Did I look dignified and classy enough? Would Eddie be proud to see me put together so *appropriately*?

Probably, but he'd also laugh at my indecision and tell me I look just as beautiful in sweatpants as a fancy dress.

When I made my way downstairs, my mom fussed over me. She was worried that I wasn't eating enough and offered me everything and anything under the sun. I ate something small to appease her and avoid the inevitable lecture.

We met at Eddie's grandmother's house, where limos arrived to take us back to the high school. This proved to be the longest, hardest drive yet. I wasn't ready to say goodbye. I wanted everything to stop but didn't know what I'd do when it was over. Right now everyone I needed was gathered together. What would I do when they all went home? I was so tired of the constant chaos and people in my face, but the silence in my future terrified me. The last thing I wanted was more time alone to think about living my life without Eddie. What did that even look like? A "normal" life? I didn't want that. I wanted Eddie.

As we pulled up to the school, I saw the fire trucks, the Patriot Guard Riders, and news vans. We'd given the reporters permission to record the ceremony as long as they promised not to come near us. There was no way I could handle being asked questions like, "How do you feel?" I'd lose it and likely say something I'd regret. As it was, I already felt like I wanted to vomit. Thankfully the protesters made the smart choice and didn't show up.

The parking lot was filled with cars and people clustered everywhere. As the limos dropped us off, we were greeted by the principal of the school. He directed us to a private room where we could sit before the services started. Once there, I looked at my mother-in-law and tried to force a smile. It was no use. We were both so tired and overcome with grief.

When it was time to enter the gym, my racing heart reminded me I was alive. Whether I wanted it or not, this was happening. Jeanine and I stood in the front with the rest of our family members behind us. Freedom Riders lined the walls, holding flags with pride. I wanted to hug each and every one of them, to smile and tell them how grateful I was, but even that was too difficult to bear. With our arms locked around each other, Jeanine and I held each other up as we walked into the packed gym and down the aisle to the front row. Fleeting eye contact was filled with such anguish that I felt like I might break at any moment.

Walking down the long, depressing aisle toward my husband, I couldn't help but think of two months prior—the different, infinitely happier circumstances of our wedding. In my elegant, white, lace dress, I'd walked toward the man of my dreams, our guests smiling as they witnessed our love. Now my white dress had turned black, and Eddie's beautiful smile had vanished, hidden inside a somber, flag-draped coffin.

I tried to avoid the faces in the crowd because I felt like I was hanging on by a single thread. The moments of eye contact filled with sorrow could make me break down in an instant. I needed to stay strong. We walked down the long aisle and sat in the front row next to the podium. I hate public speaking and feel uncomfortable in the spotlight but I felt compelled to speak at Eddie's funeral. I had to do it for him and knew he would give me the strength I needed.

An Army general spoke first and presented me and the Bolens with the Bronze Star, Purple Heart, and several other medals that had been awarded to Eddie. He spoke about the military and Eddie's sacrifice to our country. He also quoted a conversation he had with Eddie's Battalion commander in Afghanistan, who said, "He put the safety of the soldiers before himself. He never failed on any mission." Finny was going to speak as well and I figured he would go before me. As the general was speaking I heard, "And his wife Andrea Bolen would like to say a few words." I had an uneasy feeling in my stomach and felt as if the room was spinning.

"I need your help Eddie." I whispered under my breath. I slowly walked to the podium, and tried to unfold my paper as my hands were shaking uncontrollably. I couldn't look up at first but could feel all eyes on me. I could see so many faces yet still tried to avoid eye contact.

"I'm not very good at this," I began, my voice quivering. "Eddie was the one who was good at public speaking, but I'll try my best."

I looked at the coffin and then at the crowd. At the back of the room the Freedom Riders stood proudly. Their faces reminded me of my obligation and provided me with little bit of comfort. It wasn't much, but it was enough, and gave me all I needed to get through my speech.

"I always knew he was popular, but now I think he's just showing off."

With the sound of soft laughter in my ears, I felt a little more stable and slightly less uncomfortable. I took a deep breath, unfolded my speech, and began.

"I could talk about Eddie for days. The wonderful memories are endless. Most people here have at least one funny Eddie story. There was never a dull moment. He was either singing, dancing, or just being really loud and animated. The thing that people remember the most is his smile. His smile was infectious, so genuine and so full of life. He never took anything for granted and he always appreciated everything he had. He was truly one of a kind. He would give the shirt off his back to anyone who needed it—and that's when he actually wore a shirt. He would do anything for anyone, because he had a heart of gold.

Eddie was proud to serve in the military and he believed in what he was fighting for. He didn't try to be a hero; you can't try to be something that you already are. He loved his family and friends tremendously, and I know that he would not want us to mourn his death but would rather we celebrate his life. It is incredible to see the amount of lives that he has touched.

To my husband, my hero, my best friend, I will always think about our times together: the way you would sing to me, even though you were out of key; how you knew how to make me smile, just by the way you looked at me; and how you always made me laugh until I had tears in my eyes. You are a true hero and will greatly be missed by all.

Eddie, I will love you always and forever. I hope that each and every one of you can take a little piece of Eddie with you. If you're having a bad day, or are just upset about something, just think, "What would Eddie do?" It may be a little silly, but I can guarantee that it will make you laugh."

I walked over to Eddie, kissed my fingers and gently placed them on the casket. As I walked back to my seat, I kept my gaze focused on the floor. I couldn't bear to see all the tear-filled eyes. Finny walked up to the podium next with Carson trailing for support. In his usual charming and engaging way,

Finny shared memories of Eddie, and made everyone laugh when he said, "Look at the extent Eddie went to, to get school canceled yesterday. I think he would have done anything under the sun when he was in high school to get a day of school cancelled. He finally got that done." Eddie's old football coach spoke as well, expressing what an incredibly positive role model he'd been both on and off the field.

The funeral closed with a beautiful song, *You Raise Me Up,* sung by Eddie's uncle, David. The pallbearers lined up next to the casket and picked it up, placing it carefully on the pulley. Slowly, they walked the casket down the aisle as the family followed. Jeanine and I walked together, holding each other up once more. Alone, we didn't have the strength to make that walk, but together we made it.

We followed the casket through the hallway of the school, passing the Patriot Riders once again. Taking one agonizing step at a time, we managed to leave the building and painfully watched the casket being placed back into the hearse. The limos sat idling, and we gathered in them for the short ride to the cemetery, located directly behind the school. It was a fitting resting place for Eddie. He would have appreciated having the best seat in the house to watch all the football games.

We disembarked at the cemetery, stepping out into the bitter cold. The sun was shining, but its warmth was diminished by the frigid wind. Small American flags decorated the ground of the cemetery, whipping to and fro. Military personnel and the Patriot Riders proudly lined the way to the gravesite. Nearby was a small, tented area holding about twenty chairs. Floral arrangements in a multitude of colors and sizes surrounded the casket. The heart-shaped wreath I ordered was right by his side.

Jeanine and I were directed to the first two seats in the front row, and the rest of our family settled beside us. My long coat afforded me some protection from the wind, and my heavy maroon scarf did double duty as a neck warmer and tear-and-snot catcher. I don't think anyone noticed, but even if they did, I didn't care. If I closed my eyes, I could imagine it was Eddie's arms tight around me, his loving embrace keeping me warm. For brief moments, I could feel him. He was with me.

After Eddie's general said a few words, the attending soldiers gently and honorably folded an American flag into the iconic triangle. This was the moment I'd seen in the movies—it was so surreal. I couldn't believe it was happening to Eddie. Words were spoken, but I wasn't able to focus enough to decipher them. The general received the folded flag from the soldiers, then walked forward and handed it to me.

In that moment, I truly became a military widow. When my fingers curled for the first time around that flag, I felt a stabbing pain in my heart that radiated outward, like all the pieces of me were separating and crumbling to ash. It was all I could do to hold my head up as tears poured down my face.

The same flag ceremony was repeated with the same dignity and solemnity for Jeanine. We sat crying together, tightly holding our folded flags. Seven soldiers moved as one, lifting their large caliber guns to the sky. They fired once, twice, three times, each explosion jerking us in our seats. I couldn't watch the display, focusing instead on the casket until the salute was over and we were told that we could give our final goodbyes.

My feet were numb, but I slowly managed to walk to the casket, wishing everyone would just disappear and leave me alone with my husband. Hundreds of people had begun lining up, wanting to pay their final respects. I was both grateful they were there and resentful at the same time—I wanted hours with him but only had minutes.

I stood over my husband's casket, cradling the flag in my arms. I wanted to throw myself onto it. I wanted to scream. But by the skin of my teeth, I kept the pieces of me together. Tears clouded my vision before I bent down and gently kissed the casket near his head. The last kiss I would ever be able to give him.

Wet drops of tears fell on the flag that remained draped on the casket as I whispered, "I love you always and forever my love. Please stay with me."

Then I straightened, turned away, and walked back to the waiting cars. I couldn't watch anyone else say their goodbye.

*　　*　　*

The funeral reception was held at the local American Legion. Many who attended the service came, as well as retired veterans and people from the community. I felt completely exhausted, but surprisingly, a little hungry. I hadn't been able to eat much in the past ten days, but I finally felt like I needed something.

As I was getting some food to snack on, a retired veteran approached me. With tears in his eyes, he presented me with a patch representing the unit he was in. I gave him a big hug, touched by the gesture and remembering how much Eddie loved speaking to veterans. He always had such a tremendous amount of respect and admiration for them. I felt that same respect and love as I conversed with this man.

A little while later, as I sat quietly at a table with friends, I happened to glance over at the Fallen Soldier Table, a single table set up with an empty plate and a candle to honor Eddie. Clare walked up to the table and placed a cookie on the empty plate. When she saw me watching her, I couldn't help but smile. She giggled and said, "It's only appropriate, Eddie's hungry." I laughed, my heart swelling with love for Clare. Her positive attitude and outlook on life reminded me so much of Eddie.

The longest day of my life wasn't quite over. After saying farewell to those heading home, we headed to a local bar, Tin Pin. The place was packed with people remembering and celebrating Eddie. A group of about fifteen guys even wore their high school football jerseys as a tribute to Eddie. He would have loved the recognition and the gesture put a small smile on my face.

Over the course of the night, I met many people I'd only heard stories about. Many of them were Eddie's classmates from high school. People kept handing me drinks left and right, and no one would allow me to pay for anything. At one point, I tried to sneak off and pay for a drink at the bar, but even the bartender wouldn't take my money. I appreciated everyone's generosity, but nevertheless it was still a sad reminder of why we were all there. The bartender also told me that since Eddie's jersey number was forty-four, and his favorite liquor was Jack Daniels, he decided to sell shots of Jack Daniels for forty-four cents and donate the money to the Wounded Warriors. This gesture, on top of all the others, only cemented for me how giving and wonderful the people of Chittenango truly were.

Despite the comfort of being around people who loved Eddie, and the innumerable funny stories being shared, my happiness quickly diminished as the night wore on. Standing at the edge of the crowd, I looked around me. On my left, people cried and consoled each other, but on my right, people laughed and told funny stories. I knew Eddie would have wanted the latter. He would have loved people laughing and being surrounded by everyone's joy.

Eddie should have been at my side, laughing right along with me. But I'd never hear his laugh again. The realization hit me hard, and suddenly I started feeling suffocated and overwhelmed. Too many people were around me, trying to talk all at once. I could barely breathe, and I knew a panic attack was squeezing my lungs. I managed to get through the crowds and sneak out the back door. Walking around didn't help calm me. The cold air, though refreshing, did nothing to soothe my state of mind.

Leaning against a secluded wall, I tried to catch my breath. My legs weakened and I slid gracelessly to the ground. I pulled my legs in close, wrapped my arms around them, and dropped my head between my knees. Alone at last, I was coming apart, and there was nothing I could do to stop it.

The tears started flowing, gaining in intensity until I was sobbing hysterically. Every muscle and bone in my body ached. My soul felt fractured, my heart torn apart. Eddie was gone. I was alone.

After a few minutes, a gentle hand touched my shoulder. I looked up to see Carson and Ben, dear friends of Eddie's. Their presence eased a small portion of my vast loneliness. None of us spoke—there was nothing left to say. I held out my arms and they sat on either side of me, resting their heads on my shoulders. We sat together for some time, just crying and silently giving comfort. And even though my pain was still there, raw and inescapable, I knew as long as I was with the people who remembered and loved Eddie, I would never be alone.

The boys, (Ben, Eddie, Carson, Finny).

Chapter Seven

MY LAST VISIT TO FORT POLK

A large part of me never wanted to see Fort Polk again, but Major Johnston had mentioned that the commanding officers wanted to hold a ceremony for Eddie. Even though most of Eddie's unit was still deployed, there were many others who wanted to commemorate him.

The thought of being at Fort Polk without Eddie made me sick. But how could I not attend a ceremony for my husband? And truthfully, there are some people there I wanted to see—members of the extended family I'd developed during my time there. So I asked Finny, Carson, and Ben if they would come with me. They readily agreed, and Major Johnston set up their travel arrangements. Despite the painful prospect of returning to the place where Eddie and I had spent so much time together, I knew it would be healing for both me and his closest friends.

They each packed a small bag and traveled to Rockland on the Sunday after the funeral. Our flights to Louisiana were booked for Monday. We spent the evening at my parents' house, ordering food and sharing a bottle of wine. My close friend Jenna came over and we focused on keeping the mood light. I was still broken and in pieces, but their company did blunt the sharpest edges of my pain. Being with them made me feel like Eddie was there with us.

Major Johnston couldn't get us all on the same flight, leaving me with a 6:00 a.m. departure, while the guys were flying out around noon. The major would be flying with me and was due at my house at four in the morning. As the evening wound down, I reflected on how lucky I was to have the major as my casualty officer. He'd been working tirelessly over the last few weeks to make sure everything ran smoothly. Once again, my admiration grew for the steadfast loyalty found within the military.

As it neared midnight, I went upstairs to pack a bag and get ready for bed. My mom, also ready to call it a night, came up with me. We were in my room for no more than five minutes when we heard glass shatter downstairs. We traded wry glances, neither of us surprised given our rowdy company, and headed back to the kitchen.

What we saw resembled a scene from a bad horror movie. Red wine painted the walls and floor, mixing with blood pumping ceaselessly from a cut on Finny's hand. Carson was on his knees trying to wipe up the mess, but his efforts only smeared the blood further. Nearby, Finny held his bleeding hand in his shirt, trying not to drip any more blood on the floor. Ben and Jenna were standing frozen, shocked looks of horror on their faces. Once I realized no one was seriously injured, I couldn't help but laugh at the ridiculousness.

My mom began calmly giving orders. "Carson, here's another paper towel. Jenna and Ben, clean up the broken glass. Finny, come with me and put your hand over the sink." Relieved to have someone taking charge, everyone hustled to obey.

We washed the blood off Finny's hand, and the story of what happened emerged. They'd been horsing around when a wine glass had started to fall off the table. As Finny grabbed it, the glass shattered and a shard of the broken glass sliced open his thumb. Once the wound was clean, we could see that the cut was deep. From the way the blood continued to pump from the wound, we knew it must have hit an artery.

My mom and I brought him into the bathroom to clean his thumb and wrap it in gauze to slow the bleeding. Normally, Finny is the guy that you want around in any type of difficult situation. He's always calm and entertaining. But this situation was different. Even with his normal pale Irish skin tone, I'd never seen his face so white. He tried to stay composed, but I could see the uneasiness in his eyes. I assured him that the cut wasn't that bad, but as the blood continued to flow, he could see that I was lying. It was obvious he needed stitches. However, he'd just started a new job and wouldn't have health insurance until January. Fortunately, the Ophthalmologist my mom and I worked for was a surgeon. After a brief call, he agreed to meet Finny and my mom first thing in the morning to stitch up his thumb.

Meanwhile, Carson joined us in the bathroom. Unable to resist the opportunity, he began recording the whole process on his phone, complete with frank and hilarious commentary. To combat Finny's visible worry we took Carson's lead and cracked jokes until even Finny couldn't help but smile.

*   *   *

The sky was still dark and the air frigid when, at four o'clock on the dot, the major picked me up in a van issued from West Point. He was professionally dressed in his Class A's, while I looked exhausted and grungy in my sweats. My face was pale except for the dark circles of sleeplessness under my eyes. I hadn't had much rest with thoughts of returning to Fort Polk occupying my mind all night. My heart ached as I recalled that it had only been a month since I left Louisiana and the home I shared with Eddie.

Beside me, Major Johnston looked wide-awake and composed even though I knew he was just as tired as I was. Again, I felt a surge of gratitude for him. He'd been with me on every step of this heartbreaking journey. I wondered what was going through his mind . . . if he wished this could all be over. But whatever his private thoughts, I knew I wouldn't have made it through the last weeks without his steadfast presence.

From the moment we boarded the plane, the flight attendants were attentive and sweet, bumping us both to first-class seats. I'd loved hearing from Eddie about the times he was upgraded to first class. It didn't happen often, but it was nice to be reminded that people cared about our servicemen and women.

The major and I took advantage of the comfortable seats, passing out shortly after takeoff. We had a short layover in Houston, but thankfully the wait for our connecting flight was less than an hour. When we landed at Alexandria Airport my heart sank. I'd flown into that airport countless times. And every time before, Eddie was there to greet me with a huge smile and even bigger bear hug. Knowing he wouldn't be there was almost unbearable, and his absence when we disembarked reopened the fresh wound in my heart. My only relief was that we didn't linger as we took our carry-on bags and walked immediately out of the airport.

I welcomed the warm Louisiana air that breezed gently across my face, soothing my nerves. Sgt. Shane Adams greeted us and led us to a large van. I thanked him again for his kindness and for escorting Eddie from Dover. The drive to the post was about forty-five minutes. I spent the time staring out the window, replaying the numerous drives Eddie and I had made to and from the airport. When the memories became too much, I closed my eyes to hold back tears.

Once on post, Shane took us to our hotel and after checking in, Major Johnston and I parted ways to relax for a while. As soon as the door closed behind me, isolation crashed in. It was the first time I'd been truly alone in weeks. Grief surged in an unstoppable wave, buckling my knees. Leaning against the door, I felt the strength in my legs give way and slid gracelessly to the floor. Sitting there like a tear-drenched zombie, I looked into the past.

One of the times I visited Eddie, we talked about wanting to go wine tasting. Because there weren't any vineyards close by we went to the store and bought a couple bottles of wine from different places. When we returned to our hotel room, we opened the first bottle—a German wine—and looked up the vineyard online. We repeated the process with bottles from Australia and California, making up scenarios as if we were in each location.

The memory was so vivid, the love we shared so real, that I felt like I could *see* Eddie and me sitting at the small table. I heard his voice telling me that I was the best thing that had ever happened to him. I felt his lips as I leaned forward and kissed him.

A buzzing from my bag jolted me from my memories. It was a text message from Finny saying that they would make the flight on time. My mom had taken him that morning to the doctor, who confirmed that an artery had been hit. In keeping with the antics of the prior night, Finny convinced my mom to record the whole bloody process of stitching the wound closed. Laughing through my tears, I thought about how there was never a dull moment with Eddie's friends around. The event was so typical of the tightly-knit crew that when I closed my eyes, I could clearly see Eddie laughing and carrying on with them.

Until I received Finny's text, I hadn't realized just how worried I'd been that he wouldn't be able to come. His message lifted that weight from my shoulders. As long as the guys were with me, I could get through the next few days. With renewed purpose, I jumped in the shower and took care of my tear-stained face.

*   *   *

I was happy that the guys would be able to see what our life had been like at Fort Polk as well as meet some of our friends who were still there. They were especially excited when we brought them to the drive-through Daiquiri Station. Eddie had described the spots so vividly that they were anxious to see them. They weren't disappointed.

Thanksgiving was approaching and many of the soldiers had gone home for R&R. The service that took place on post was a lot smaller than the one in Chittenango, but no less dignified. They provided pamphlets with Eddie's picture on it, and the contributors all did a beautiful job paying tribute to my husband. One of the speakers was Eddie's roommate and close friend from Fort Polk, Sergeant Cary Davis. I was proud of him for his heartfelt words honoring his dear friend because I knew from my own experiences how difficult that task was.

After he was finished I couldn't take in any more. I could hear the chaplain speaking, but his words bounced off my ears. Shane signaled to me that it was time to walk up to the picture of Eddie and have my moment alone. He held out his arm and I locked mine around his. As we walked, my heart began to race. The moment Shane started to step back, I clenched my fingers tighter on his arm and whispered, "Please don't leave me alone up here." Nodding in understanding, he stayed.

The large photograph of Eddie didn't look like him at all. It looked more like a mugshot. He was unsmiling, and I vaguely remembered him telling me he was hungover when it was taken. The image didn't represent my joyful, smiling husband. I barely stayed a minute before walking away. I could feel the weight of everyone's eyes on me but I couldn't look back.

*   *   *

That evening we gathered at a local bar, and although we had a good time shooting pool, drinking, and telling stories, it felt like a repeat of the night of Eddie's funeral. How long could we keep doing this? Half of me wanted these nights to never stop while the other half wanted to run far, far away.

One thing I knew for certain—I didn't want to be in Louisiana anymore. It was too painful to see all the places Eddie and I used to spend our time. I wanted to be back in New York, back with my family. That night I stayed at Shane's house with the guys. His family was in Mississippi for Thanksgiving, and he was nice enough to let me stay in his son's room.

As I buried my face in the pillow, I longed for a dreamless sleep, but my wish went unfulfilled. Every time I closed my eyes I was back in Afghanistan. I could see Eddie, so close and yet so impossibly far. I yelled and screamed but no sound came out. I tried to run to him, but my legs wouldn't move. Then he vanished. I dreamed different versions of the same nightmare over and over, but the ending was the same. Eddie always vanished, disappearing before my eyes.

I stood alone, clouds of smoke and ash billowing around me.

Chapter Eight

THE WIDOW

I used to associate pain as being primarily physical. Now that I've endured the reality of internal pain, however, I know physical pain pales in comparison. Emotional suffering runs deep and darkens the soul. It's pain that cannot be seen, but is nevertheless real and experienced every day.

My pain starts in my heart, flows through my brain, and spreads throughout my body. Some days it's hot as fire, boiling my blood and triggering instant rage. A moment later, I'm cold as ice and just as numb. But the sadness is the hardest. When depression takes over, it's difficult to escape. When I'm angry or numb, at least I know the feelings will pass. Depression doesn't. I'm caught in its grip, with nowhere to go, nowhere to turn.

When I find myself in that dark, limitless place, and overwhelmed by hopelessness, Eddie saves me. His memory comes to my rescue and helps guide me out. Until the next time I fall. But no matter how smothering my sadness, how deep my depression, my heart knows he will always come. He won't let me be lost in that bottomless hole.

The closest anyone's come to explaining exactly how I feel is my cousin, Michael, who lost his girlfriend many years ago when he was just sixteen. His words stuck with me, and I use them to remind myself I'm not alone.

"Fuckers will say, time heals all wounds. That statement is cliché and tactless. We heal with pink-ribbon scars that never forget, and that's okay. It's the way it's supposed to be. Eddie is going to be a part of your heart for the rest of your life. He will always be with you in that way. You'll recover, but the scars will remain. I'm not one hundred percent sure we ever fully heal. Those scars tell our story. They keep the memory alive. They change us, often for the better."

*   *   *

After returning home from the memorial in Louisiana, the craziness of the preceding weeks began to subside. I was able to spend more time alone, away from watchful, worried eyes. But my newfound freedom was a mixed blessing. I spent a lot of time in bed, crying for hours until finally sleep claimed me. Nightmares became an almost nightly struggle. I dreamed over and over again of the explosion that had taken Eddie's life.

Depression had me firmly in its clutches. I didn't want to take my life, but I didn't want to live anymore. I wanted to be with Eddie. A world without him wasn't a world I wanted to endure. I began fantasizing about being with Eddie again, wondering who would come to my funeral, who would speak, and who would eventually forget about me. I became more reckless, driving irrationally when no one else was on the road, doing things I would normally fear because I was no longer afraid. I didn't care enough to be scared. I didn't care about my health and drank a lot. Sometimes with others but also by myself. My fear of heights seemed to disappear. I fantasized about dying and escaping from the pain.

As often as possible I lost myself in memories of the past. Back in a world Eddie lived in, I replayed our life together like a movie reel. Details were incredibly vivid, from smells to thoughts. I needed a break from reality. I preferred living in my fantasy world where Eddie and I were together because my reality no longer made sense. I didn't know the face I saw in mirrors. The reflection was a stranger to me, a woman with tired, empty eyes. Every facet of life took new effort. It hurt to smile, to laugh, it even hurt to breathe. There were days I woke up from dreams of Eddie alive and well, and they were so real that my heart would shatter all over again.

Nights and mornings were the hardest. Every night in bed I'd picture myself back in the apartment with Eddie. The last one to get into bed would usually swan dive onto the other person. He would wrap his arms around me and pull me close. No matter how close we were, he'd tell me I wasn't close enough. There was no better feeling in the world than being in his arms. Feeling his lips on my cheek and neck. Having him whisper in my ear how much he loved me. The idea of falling asleep knowing that the love of my life was there, and tomorrow we'd spend another day belonging to each other, was everything. Every night, my husband was still with me. But every morning, he was gone.

When I awoke, I'd open my eyes hoping to find Eddie lying beside me. Then my hand would search and find only emptiness where he should be. Other mornings, I lingered between sleep and waking, struggling to figure out if his death had just been a horrible dream. I often woke up in the middle of the night, sweating and crying out for him. Nightmares haunted me with images of his life being taken away. Happy visions of his smiling face taunted me before vanishing.

About a month after Eddie's death, I went to the gynecologist for my yearly checkup. I knew I wasn't pregnant, and yet the grief in me wanted to believe it was possible, that there was still a chance I could have his child. Even though Eddie wanted to start a family right away, I wanted to wait for him to return from Afghanistan. When the midwife told me I wasn't pregnant, my heart sank. The child we fantasized about would never be.

On Facebook, the notifications were endless. Heartfelt condolences poured in every day, as well as hundreds of friend-requests. The amount of attention I was receiving was overwhelming. At least when it came to social media, I could easily sign out and escape. Harder by far was the constant stream of mail. Every day I received sympathy cards, and even gifts. My phone buzzed with text messages and new voicemails at least a few times every hour. For the most part I saved the voicemails for later listening, but when I saw one from the supervisor at my former internship, some instinct guided me to listen to it.

After offering condolences, she made it clear that she'd love to have me come back during the next semester. The last time we spoke, I told her I wouldn't be returning to school, but it was still sweet of her to extend the invitation. That night in bed, I thought more about the voicemail. How was I supposed to live a normal life? Feeling the way I felt now, was finishing school even possible?

My answer came from an unsurprising but profound source—a memory of Eddie. Over dinner one night before his final deployment, I expressed how much admiration I had for what he was doing. He smiled softly and in his usual humble way, told me that what he was doing was nothing compared to me getting a master's degree. He was always so proud of the fact that I was bound and determined to go to graduate school. While I thought it was crazy to compare the two, I appreciated his endless support.

I'd be lying if I said that I immediately reenrolled in classes. But for the first time, the idea of finishing school didn't seem so impossible. Eddie believed in me, in my career choice to be a school counselor, and I didn't want to let him down. With only two semesters of classes and internships to go, I could actually see myself graduating. I could feel Eddie's pride and satisfaction at this accomplishment.

The dining room table at my parents' house looked like the backroom of a post office, and the time came when I couldn't ignore it anymore. I sat down and began tackling the exorbitant pile, reading letters from people in the community, military personnel, family members, and even people Eddie went to school with. I could feel the love in the words, as well as the respect they had for Eddie and the military. The letters I enjoyed the most were those expressing gratitude for his sacrifice, and those from people close to him that included funny stories about how he touched their lives. All the words, no matter how sterile or meaningful, served to remind me what kind of man my husband was and why I'd fallen in love with him.

One of the most touching letters was from one of my high school friends.

Hey Andrea,

My heart is absolutely broken for you. I've been trying all weekend to think of how to fully express my sorrow for your loss but there really are no words. I'm so happy that I was able to be there for your special day, seeing you two together made me believe in true love all over again. I barely got to know Eddie but the way he looked at you that night made me love him. He saw the beautiful light in you that we have all known since we were just youngins. What I really want to say is don't let this turn that light out. I can't even imagine the pain, anger, regret, etc. that is going through you at the moment but don't let it turn the light out. You are one of the sweetest, most endearing, special people that I have the pleasure of having in my life and seeing any part of that fade away would just be a shame. Honor his memory and continue to live your life to the fullest, I know this is what he would have wanted. Don't let this make you bitter, continue to be that amazing soul that Eddie fell in love with in the first place.

Your friend,
Chris

I read the letter several times and really thought about his beautiful words. They made me question the person I'd become. The "light" he referred to was gone. Before, I considered myself a happy, optimistic woman. But now, I didn't know if I could ever be that person again. I felt like that part of me died the day the soldiers first came to my house, leaving a bitter, angry, and depressed shell of a person behind. Finding new happiness felt impossible. My friend clearly had faith that I could be that person again, but I wasn't so sure.

The following day I received a text message from a family friend, Liz Pagnani. She introduced the idea of holding a package-drive for the soldiers in Eddie's platoon and wanted to make sure I would be okay with it. I thought it sounded amazing and gave her the address to send the packages to. She of course invited me to come, but I wasn't sure I could face everyone. It wasn't until the night before the event that I decided to go.

Liz and her family did a wonderful job planning and executing the event. They set up five tables, each one with a different picture of Eddie and labeled with basic needs like toiletries, food, and entertainment. The outpouring of donations and support was incredible. Donations allowed for the creation of so many packages that the organizers decided to send out twenty a week. Now the men would receive care packages for the next several months. It was inspiring to see how many people wanted to not only do whatever they could to help our troops overseas, but also keep Eddie's memory alive.

Not long after, another opportunity arose to celebrate Eddie's life for a good cause. A friend of Eddie's from high school, Nick, wanted to put together a charity golf tournament. I knew nothing about golf tournaments but absolutely loved the idea. I immediately knew which charities I wanted to donate to. Wounded Warriors is an incredible foundation that helps wounded soldiers returning from war. I personally knew of men from Eddie's platoon who received help from the foundation. I also wanted to donate to the Fisher House, the amazing charity that helped with my transportation and hotel stays after Eddie's death. They also covered the cost of the flights for the fellow military wives who flew in to accompany me for the services, as well as flights for Eddie's friends to Fort Polk.

We decided Memorial Day weekend would be a perfect weekend to have the tournament. Nick put together a Facebook page to notify people of the date and details. We also took advantage of the public forum to maintain interest in sending packages overseas to the deployed troops. Anyone could join and help plan the tournament, assist with donations, or just spread the word about the event to others. A lot of people stepped forward to help with various tasks. As more and more people signed up, I was thrilled, knowing the event would have a huge turnout—just like Eddie would have wanted it.

One afternoon I was browsing all the lovely comments on the page, many from people who didn't even know Eddie, when one comment hit me like a punch. A woman I didn't know had posted to ask if anyone knew the address she should send care packages to. Right below it, another woman had replied with four little words that ricocheted through my heart.

"Just ask the widow."

There it was—the truth—right in front of me. The world around me stopped, transforming my identity as Andrea Bolen into a nameless widow.

Although I'd been referred to as a widow during the ceremonies, for some reason this woman's comment hit me really hard. Perhaps it was the months that had passed, or the fact that I was slowly, torturously working to pull myself out of the pit of depression and grief. Whatever it was, in that moment I was no longer a person. Not a wife. Not a woman.

Just a widow.

Chapter Nine

GOING THROUGH THE MOTIONS

Returning to work was a big challenge. While my coworkers knew what had happened, many of the patients only knew that I'd recently been married. I had worked there for a long time, and was friendly with the patients I saw often. I dreaded their well-meaning questions about how life was going as a married woman. My boss understood my distress, and kindly allowed me to work at the front desk instead of with patients. I was so grateful for that. Some days, I made it through my shift without falling apart. Other days, I escaped to the bathroom to cry in private.

On one of the more difficult days, I made the mistake of stepping outside to answer a phone call. The building houses multiple doctors' offices, and patients came and went. As my conversation ended, I glanced down the hallway and saw a woman I recognized as the mother of one of my high school classmates. The second she saw me, I braced myself for what was going to happen next. Sobbing, she ran toward me and threw her arms around me in a powerful embrace. I just stood there, frozen until she was done, before I said goodbye and returned to work.

Receiving sympathy from virtual strangers had become commonplace in my life. Unfortunately, I wasn't able to handle every instance with grace. Grief, I'd come to learn, was in some ways an intensely private experience. These strangers didn't know Eddie like I knew him. No one understood what was going through my mind. And while sharing my sorrow with friends and family was comforting, the constant pressure from the larger community wore me down. Every comment about how hard the holidays would be or how he's in a better place ignited more resentment than gratitude. Despite best intentions, sympathizing was one thing, but slicing me apart, that was another.

Of course, I can't speak for everyone who's lost a spouse or someone close. I'm sure others have different experiences. But for me, I felt that my grief was mine to share when I wanted to do so, not simply because someone spotted me at the gym or a parking lot. I soon discovered that many people didn't know how to speak to someone who's grieving. Some even believed it would benefit me to hear about all the horrible things that had happened in their lives. While I felt terrible for their losses, there was only so much grief one person could bear. I knew people were trying to relate to me, but I was already lost in my deep, dark world. I needed something positive to hold on to, not more darkness.

People told me about losses of loved ones, or a friend of a friend who lost someone. I heard about horrible car accidents, illnesses, and some even compared my loss to the loss of an inanimate object. Something that was never living or breathing! A woman sent me a message saying her biggest fear was having her husband come home the same way Eddie did. I can confidently say that's most military wives' worst fear. Others had the nerve to ask if I was dating again so shortly after burying my husband.

Going to the grocery store was like walking into emotional battle. I always ran into at least one person I knew. Sometimes they looked at me with surprise and told me how great I looked, like it was a miracle I was showered and didn't have food in my hair. And once, I even had a stranger recognize me from the newspaper and ask if I was the girl who lost her husband in Afghanistan. As if I needed to be reminded! There is no rulebook for how to deal with situations like that. Before I could tell her to take her pity and shove it, I muttered an affirmative and walked away.

The most absurd and infuriating response I received occurred a month after Eddie passed. A woman accused me of having an affair with her husband because he'd been reaching out to me from time to time. I had so many wonderful people checking in on me, especially my military friends. I tried to figure out what universe I was in at that moment because part of me felt like I was in the twilight zone. It was bizarre, heartless and infuriating.

There's one more instance of misplaced sympathy for me that will go down in the books as one of the most absurd. "I know what it's like to lose the one thing that's most important to you. It wasn't a person in my case, but when lacrosse was taken from me, a part of me died. I will never forget it. It was my one true love and passion." That's ten seconds of ignorance I will remember forever.

So many times, I fielded comments that were nearly incomprehensible. I began journaling about them just to get them out of my head. This habit came in handy one evening when a dear friend of mine put her foot in her mouth. She came over to spend some time with me and the conversation naturally turned to Eddie. I brought up all the ridiculous things people had been saying to me, when out of the blue she said, "I truly believe that God only gives people things they can handle."

Instead of my normal reaction of annoyance, I laughed and went upstairs to grab my journal. I found the page I wanted and showed it to my friend. She started reading some of the entries aloud, her expression slowly becoming wide-eyed with shock.

"You're young, you'll find another husband. I know exactly how you feel. My dog died last year. God only takes the good ones. I don't know how you keep on living." And finally, she came to, "God doesn't give you more than you can handle."

As her horrified eyes lifted to mine, I laughed. "See?"

Her face turned red with embarrassment. "Oh crap, I made the book! I'm so sorry!"

I grinned. "Now you know what *not* to say." We both had a good laugh.

*   *   *

I finally began to burn out from all the obligations, opening letters, fielding public condolences from random people and having to deal with the worry from friends and family about being alone. My sister was living in Buffalo at the time, so I booked a plane ticket for a three-day weekend together. I desperately needed her comfort and to get the hell out of Rockland. When the plane landed, I didn't even care that it was freezing cold with at least a foot of snow on the ground. We spent the weekend in her cozy apartment, hanging out and watching movies.

At some point, we started talking about Eddie. The conversation eventually turned to our beliefs about whether people hang around even after they pass away. I shared with her all the times I've felt him close to me. Before my own experience, I'd always been skeptical about loved ones staying with us. But that was also before I lost someone so incredibly close to me.

Eddie didn't only visit me in my dreams. There were times I would be in a room by myself and I'd get a strong whiff of his cologne, as though he was right beside me. One day in particular, I'd just finished a session with one of my clients. The session went well but I was running on little sleep due to my recurring nightmares. As I left the building and started walking toward my car, memories flooded my tired mind. Tears filled my eyes and I rushed the rest of the way. Once inside, I closed my eyes and began to cry.

"Eddie, I'm trying so hard to make you proud of me. I don't know if I can do this. I need you!" All I could do was whisper over and over, "I need you Eddie, I need you."

So he came.

Over the sound of my weeping, I heard Eddie's ringtone, *Smile* by Uncle Kracker. I looked at the dark face of my phone, and realized it wasn't ringing. The radio was off and my keys were still in my hand. Against all logic, the song kept playing. Eventually my tears subsided and I smiled.

"Thank you Eddie," I told the empty air. "I know you're still looking out for me. I miss you so much!" When the song ended, I felt stable enough to drive home.

As I told Diana about that occasion along with a few others, the lamp in her bedroom suddenly clicked on, casting a warm glow into the living room where we sat. Similarly shocked, we smiled at each other, goosebumps all over our bodies.

"Hi Eddie," Diana said.

That weekend with my sister brought me clarity in more ways than one. I was deeply unhappy and something in my life needed to change. I contemplated quitting work and moving in with my sister. The idea of a new life where no one knew me was very appealing. It was also unrealistic. I wasn't sure exactly how to move forward.

I did a lot of thinking on the way home, and came to the conclusion that somewhere along the line I stopped doing things for me and started doing things for Eddie. With the admission that this wasn't likely to change anytime soon, I decided I might as well continue trying to make my husband proud. I was going to reenroll in school. Not for me or for my future, but for Eddie.

The following day I called my former supervisor and asked her if the offer still stood for me to return to my internship at Camp Venture. She was very pleased and said she would love for me to come back. After I hung up I nearly vomited from the anxiety of returning to my old routine. But since I was doing it for Eddie, there was no turning back.

The holiday season was already going to be tough with Eddie deployed. This new reality was infinitely harder. I wanted nothing to do with celebrating and so-called good cheer. Holiday cards made me unreasonably angry, as did the nonstop Christmas music on the radio and heartwarming movies on television. Cards, letters, and gifts continued to arrive. While I knew they were sent with good intentions, I wanted it to stop. Every note of sympathy, book on coping with grief, or collection of military poems was a blow to my psyche—I was covered in imaginary wounds.

I never felt so alone. My friends and family still had their loved ones with them. They were sleeping with their spouse or loved one at night and waking up in their arms. Something I could no longer do. I was very happy for my friends who had someone special, but it was hard for me to see it. It was something I once had and it was ripped away from me. Eddie and I had shared the kind of love that people dream about. Now I was left with so much anger and misery that it was too much for me to witness their love and affection. I was bitter toward love and furious at the world.

Whenever I was invited out, my knee-jerk response was always *No, thank you.* Then I would think about it. If I thought I could get through it without breaking down, I'd show up. I was trying so hard to function with my life in pieces around my feet. So many people reached out to me during that time, wanting to include me in social gatherings and do nice things for me. I was truly grateful for their kindness, but there came a point when the feeling of being a charity case became overwhelming. I was tired of thanking people for their efforts to pull me toward a world I wanted no part in.

My only holiday decoration was a small, beautifully handmade Christmas tree, and two ornaments. They were all given to me by one of my oldest friends and her mother. One of the ornaments was a delicate white ball with angel wings and the other was a soldier. Both bore Eddie's name. It was an extremely thoughtful and beautiful gift. I decided to keep the tree in my room, not because I wanted to celebrate Christmas, but because Eddie would want me to. Needless to say, I was relieved when the Christmas season was finally over. I didn't have to think about how difficult it was, knowing I would never spend another Christmas with my husband.

*   *   *

I visited Eddie's burial site in Chittenango as much as I could. Eventually, I could no longer put off my final widow's task of selecting a headstone. Knowing I couldn't do it alone, I called the three men I knew would stand by me. Finny, Ben, and Carson came with me to help pick one out.

As we pulled into the parking lot, we immediately noticed the seven-foot eagle standing right in front. "That's the one!" yelled the guys. I couldn't help but laugh because it was so appropriate for Eddie. The eagle was massive and made quite a statement. We ventured inside, the laughter soothing my raw heart.

The saleswoman who helped us design the headstone was very sweet and patient with us. We were all able to participate in the final decision of what type of stone would be used, its shape, and the final, heartfelt words that would be engraved forever on its surface. Eddie would have been very happy with what we picked, even if it wasn't the seven-foot eagle.

Days later, I received a phone call from Major Johnston. Apparently, after Eddie's death, a few carpenters working in Afghanistan had made a shadow box in his memory. One of the men was from Rochester, New York, and was returning home for R&R. Major Johnston told me the carpenter wanted to personally deliver the shadow box. I was shocked and honored that this man wanted to take time out of his vacation to drive over eight hours to give me Eddie's box.

When the day arrived, I left work early. I was a little anxious about meeting this complete stranger who had done something so caring and thoughtful for me. I didn't know how he would approach me. *Would he give me words of advice? Was he there when Eddie died? I know he's not a soldier, but did he know my husband?*

I arrived home to find the man already speaking with my parents in the dining room. With kindness and humility, he introduced himself and offered condolences. His name, ironically, was Ed. He didn't ask me questions or offer advice, and I really appreciated his respect. We sat around the dining table and his story unfolded. He'd been working as a carpenter in Afghanistan and although he didn't know my husband personally, he and a few other men had wanted to make me a shadow box. It was the first one they'd ever made for a widow, but unfortunately nowhere near the last. Ed had transported the special item as his carry-on while traveling home, and his wife had graciously stained the wood.

The shadow box was beautifully handcrafted and much larger and heavier than I expected. It was twenty-one inches wide, two feet tall, and a foot deep. Behind the glass was a photo of Eddie surrounded by the medals he had earned, his Airborne pin, a few Battalion coins, and his dog tags. Ed opened the box to show me a laminated paper that bore pictures of the coins as well as their individual meanings. Then he handed me an ammo can. Inside was a booklet made from the nametags of the men in Eddie's unit. The one at the very top read *Bolen*.

A tear rolled down my cheek as I read the familiar names. These were men I spent time with while living in Louisiana, barbecuing and hanging out at the lake. This was my military family—I felt them surrounding me, sharing my pain of losing Eddie. I could feel the love they had put into making the box.

Ed stayed a little longer. At his request, my mom took a picture of us holding the box so he could show it to the men who helped build it. Grateful and honored, I put aside my self-consciousness for the photo. It didn't matter that my scrubs from work had a wacky design on them or that my hair was a mess. What mattered was the incredible compassion and sacrifice of time made on my behalf.

I couldn't visit Chittenango as much as I wanted to, so in the following weeks and months I used the shadow box as a personal headstone for Eddie. I would sit before it and talk to him. Whatever the circumstances of the day—good or bad—I found comfort in telling Eddie what was going on. Often, I'd flip through the nametags and thank each and every one of the men, and then I'd ask Eddie to watch over them and keep them safe.

*   *   *

The time finally came when my husband's belongings were ready to be returned to me. Days after Eddie's death, in the midst of a cyclone of paperwork, Major Johnston asked me if I wanted Eddie's belongings cleaned before they were delivered home. Recalling comments on a website for military widows about the anger they felt when their husbands' belongings came back smelling of laundry detergent, I told Major Johnston no. I wanted whatever remained of my husband's scent. After thinking about it, however, I realized the condition his gear must be in. Sweaty and filled with sand and dirt. I didn't want any remnants of Afghanistan, the place where my husband lost his life. I already had his cologne and the bulk of his clothing, as well as mementos and his favorite baseball hat. I called the major back and told him I changed my mind.

The day of the delivery, a familiar knot of dread sat in my stomach. This was the last of Eddie's items I would be receiving. The last of his belongings that he had with him in life. I wasn't sure I was ready—*how can anyone be ready for a moment like this?* But I also desperately wanted anything that was left of him.

Major Johnston arrived with four heavy, industrial bins which he hauled downstairs to the basement at my request. When he was gone, I sat in the basement and stared at them. Memories of helping Eddie pack for his deployment cycled through my mind. Every time I tried to approach the bins, something held me back. They were mocking me, taunting me with all they represented—they were here and Eddie wasn't. Repelled, I backed away and hurried up the basement stairs.

Halfway up, I stopped dead in my tracks as a vision of hope consumed me. Eddie and I had never spoken about a final letter in case anything was to happen to him. Had we, I probably would have thought it was morbid and told him he wouldn't need it. But at that moment, I knew there was a slight possibility that I could have one final letter from my husband. I turned around and ran to the bins. After a few deep breaths, I opened the latches on each and threw back the lids.

Everything was neatly packed. His uniforms were perfectly folded, his socks rolled in balls and many items were stored in black pouches. When I came across his camera, excitement tingled in my body. "Please, let there be pictures on it," I begged aloud. Even though he was only in Afghanistan for two weeks, I wanted to see snapshots of his final days. Holding my breath, I put the memory card and batteries back in the camera. Eight photos were on the card. Some of Eddie alone, and some of him with the soldiers in his unit. As much as I hated that Afghanistan was the last place he saw before he died, I was so grateful to have a few new pictures of my husband.

In my search for a letter, I examined every single item. I ran my fingers all over the bottom and corners to make sure nothing was hidden. I found pictures of us, some from our wedding and a few other favorites. I found his brand-new boots he didn't get a chance to wear and examined his gear and tools he used, notepads, and pens. I could picture him using everything. I found some personal items such as his e-reader, his watch, and my large FDNY T-shirt. It was my softest, oldest shirt, and he'd taken it with him to use as a pillowcase so he could feel like I was with him.

After going through every inch of the bins, my heart squeezed in pain. There was no letter, no final word, no goodbye or message of encouragement. I sat in a circle of his belongings, tears in my eyes, and did the only thing I could think to do. I talked to Eddie.

"It seems like we were just going through your items to pack. We just bought these damn boots that you didn't even get a chance to wear. I'm so angry this happened to you. This hole in my heart feels like it's getting bigger and bigger. I miss you so much and wish we were back at our apartment unpacking together."

Immediately, I felt relief. I realized I didn't need a letter to know what he would have written. My positive, full-of-life husband wouldn't want me to be in pain. He would want me to find happiness. But I didn't know how to do that when I was filled with so much grief and anger.

Maybe someday, Eddie.

I put some of the items aside to keep and packed the rest back in the bins. With time, I decided to let his friends go through them and take what they wanted. Whatever remained, I would donate to West Point.

*   *   *

In some ways, New Year's Eve wasn't as painful as Christmas but more painful in others. Just two years ago I'd been waiting so eagerly for Eddie to come home for R&R. Our New Year's kiss had come a few days late that year. Now it would be a lifetime late.

Wanting more than anything to be around the people who understood, I spent the holiday with the guys at Finny's house in Rochester. When we were all together, I always felt like a part of Eddie was there with us. Diana drove down from Buffalo and a few other friends joined us. My friend Jenna drove with me, and we spent the five-hour drive chatting mostly about inconsequential things. And, of course, my ongoing struggle to find normalcy. I found myself admitting aloud for the first time some of my biggest fears.

"Everyone has been so wonderful and there for me, but I feel like there's going to be a time when they just don't want to hear about my problems anymore. It's not like I want to talk about it all the time, but I'm not happy and it's exhausting trying to force myself to smile every day."

Jenna's expression was aghast. "Dre, no one expects you to force a smile. We know you're hurting and we *want* to be there for you."

"I know," I assured her. "But don't you think people are sick of hanging out with the depressed girl? I do, and honestly, I don't blame them."

"If people feel that way, then they're not your friends."

I wanted so badly to believe her. Maybe the truth was simpler than I thought. Maybe I wasn't afraid of people getting sick of me—maybe I was sick of myself.

The night was rowdy and fun, with multiple toasts to Eddie. I was able to enjoy myself right up until a few minutes to midnight before the panic took hold. My heart started racing and the room was spinning. I wasn't sure if it was the tequila in my system, or the dawning realization that a new year was about to begin. A new year that Eddie wouldn't be alive to see.

Everyone crowded around the television and started the countdown. I felt like I couldn't breathe. I wanted to run but Diana wrapped a supportive arm around me. When the ball dropped and everyone cheered, I was finally able to make my way outside. It was bitterly cold, but I finally felt like I could draw a full breath. The sky was shockingly clear, lit up by countless stars. Tilting my head back to take in the beauty, I whispered, "Happy New Year, my love."

It was 2011, and Eddie was still gone.

Chapter Ten

BREAKING POINT

Two months later the sympathy cards and letters were still pouring in. My phone rang upwards of twenty times a day, and I received innumerable emails and Facebook messages. The support was amazing, a buffer I relied on during my darkest days. But it also felt like a spotlight constantly followed me, marking me forever as the Widow.

Reporters were still calling me, looking for interviews, while other people wanted to know where to send packages to the troops. Every day people reached out to me for information about what they could do to help. My friends at Fort Polk were planning to host a golf tournament on Memorial Day weekend back in Louisiana. My father-in-law's company was organizing another tournament in California and I was informed that a girl I went to high school with wanted to set up a fundraiser in Eddie's name. And in my hometown of Rockland, they wanted to hold a memorial for those who hadn't been able to make the services in Syracuse.

Between work, fielding nonstop calls, emails and texts, my head was close to popping off. Added to the mix were daily instances of people asking after my wellbeing and showering me with platitudes about my loss. I could feel myself nearing the same breaking point I'd reached just months prior. I wanted to run away and hide from it all.

I tried so hard to stay strong while simultaneously feeling like everyone was waiting for me to fall apart. I developed severe social anxiety. Whenever someone mentioned Eddie's name, my muscles became tense and I could feel my throat close. I was afraid to open my mouth, afraid I would scream and sob instead of speak. I was terrified of showing vulnerability before strangers or acquaintances. I didn't want their comfort—didn't want to be smothered by it more than I already was.

One night, I had to go to the drugstore to buy a birthday card for a friend. It was only a five-minute drive, but driving had also become difficult. My mind was always filled with Eddie, but on this particular drive, instead of comfort, the happy memories hit me like a sledgehammer. In an instant I was thrown back in time to that fateful drive when my mother had called and told me to come home. To the soldiers' faces as they delivered the news. To the moment my life disintegrated.

Sobbing and hyperventilating, I could barely see the road. I managed to pull over safely and open my door for fresh air. The next thing I knew, I was vomiting on the side of the road. After what felt like hours, but was probably only minutes, I got my breathing under control. I sat in my car on the side of the road, crying as I wiped vomit off my face and thought of all the people who told me how strong I was.

In this moment, I never felt weaker.

*   *   *

The start of the semester was quickly approaching. I couldn't help but feel terrified the closer it got. I'd been avoiding places where I would see people I knew from school, and I had no doubt that my return would bring a lot of unwanted attention. Being at work was horrible enough. Some patients would see my wedding rings and ask about my husband. I would ignore the questions or give vague answers. I wouldn't discuss my personal life. I couldn't concentrate and hated speaking to people. I was easily frustrated and angry all the time. The worst was meeting new people. New people meant more questions I didn't want to answer.

With my dark frame of mind firmly in place, the first week of school was every bit as horrible as I imagined. Unlike phone calls and cards in the mail, I couldn't ignore everyone who wanted to hug me and offer sympathy face-to-face. As the usual rounds of introductions progressed, I tuned out all the stories of happy holidays and personal celebrations.

Whenever possible I stayed away from people I knew. My main goal was as simple as getting through each class. Unfortunately, because of the small class size, I couldn't hide in the back row.

Attending a school full of people wanting to become counselors was my personal recipe for disaster. Well-meaning classmates wanted to dig through my head and test their newfound skills on my brokenness. I was their number-one target. Although I couldn't necessarily blame them, I also wanted to give them stern lessons on what *not* to say to someone drowning in grief.

My breaking point came in a group counseling class. The environment was intimate and entailed a lot of hands-on work with each other. There was no way I'd be able to make it through this one class, let alone the entire semester of classes.

Alone at night, I sobbed in bed and fantasized about being with Eddie, being away from this pain-filled world. Every time I turned on the television for distraction, I saw something that triggered more tears. One night I flipped to a new show called "Coming Home," belatedly realizing it was about military personnel surprising their families. That was the final straw. I turned off the television and sat in the darkness, staring at nothing. I wanted to hide from the pain, hide from the memories, and hide from my emptiness.

The next day I woke up and felt like I'd lost my mind. I wondered if this was how someone with the beginning stages of Alzheimer's felt—like their mind was in one place and their body stuck in another. My thoughts were erratic and without clarity. I began to forget things. In the mirror was a woman I still didn't recognize, with lines of suffering across her forehead. It was her—the Widow. I had to get rid of her. I needed to do something different. With that thought, I decided to chop off my long hair to shoulder length. Though the notion of taking scissors to do it myself was appealing, I had enough sanity left to go to a salon.

My stylist was incredibly sweet to me. She offered condolences but didn't follow up with words of advice or leading questions. I was so grateful for her tact. After telling her what I wanted, I closed my eyes and let her go to work. Pieces of me were being cut away, and it was hard not to feel guilty. Eddie had loved playing with my long hair and loved it when I would wear it down. But I also knew he'd understand why I needed the change. The person I'd been—the woman he loved—had been overtaken by the Widow. With Eddie gone, I couldn't be the old Andrea anymore. Maybe instead, I could be someone new.

*   *   *

One night in February, I found the courage to attend a friend's birthday celebration in the city. She planned for a group to meet for drinks at her place, and then head out to the bars. Despite my ongoing struggle with social anxiety, I pulled myself together. So many friends had shown up for me recently, the least I could do was try to show up for them. I even bought a new dress, figuring if I looked good maybe I would feel good.

My efforts backfired spectacularly.

By the time the party reached the bars, the alcohol had been flowing for hours. I tried my best to have fun, and for a while I did. I was at the bar chatting with a friend when one of the partygoers approached us. He was clearly tipsy and kept telling me how beautiful I looked. Not until his hand slowly caressed my leg did I realize he was hitting on me. I was so shocked and angry I couldn't even formulate words. This was a man who'd known Eddie! I couldn't believe this guy's nerve. My husband had been dead

117

less than four months, and I was in no shape to start dating or even *think* about becoming romantically involved with anyone. So I did the only thing I could and walked away. Luckily, a few other friends were also ready to go, and I hitched a ride with them back to Rockland.

Diana was my go-to person for venting. We even developed a code for our conversations. Knowing how much I hated people asking, "How are you?" she'd ask what kind of day I was having. Some days were better than others, but at this point they were all difficult. There were days I was so depressed that I was nauseous. On hard days I would tell Diana it was a "vomit day," and the worst days were labeled "projectile vomit" days. It was gross, but perfectly summed up how I felt. It also gave us a laugh. I just had to say, "Today is a vomit day," and she knew exactly what I meant.

After the incident at the party, she was the first person I called.

"I feel like I'm completely losing my mind. I can't stand being around people. I hate that everyone is watching my every move. I want to disappear. If I wasn't in school, I would move away in a second. I wish more than anything it was an option."

Saying the words aloud only magnified my need for escape. I wanted to go somewhere far enough away that no one could reach me. I didn't want to answer any phone calls, texts, or emails, or have to worry about people asking me how I was doing. And maybe, just maybe, I could find a place where I could relax and just be me.

"I'm going on vacation," I told Diana. "Somewhere tropical. Alone."

"Absolutely not! You're not going to a tropical island to sulk by yourself. I'm coming with you! It will be a relaxing, sister-getaway."

She was literally the only person in the world I would want to come. With anyone else, I'd feel like I had to put on a happy face so they'd have a good time. With Diana, I didn't have to put on an act. Plus, she knew me better than anyone and would see right through it anyway. We decided on Cancun and booked a five-night, all-inclusive stay at a resort for the end of March.

Having something to look forward to made the next month and a half bearable. When our departure date finally arrived, I was beyond ready to take a break from my life. Mom dropped us off at the airport, and we headed through security. Although I was excited to leave, my mood was subdued. Airports would always be hard for me. My relationship with Eddie had involved so many flights to visit each other in our respective states. The knowledge that I would never take another trip to see him, never see his wide smile or waiting arms ready for me to leap into, was at the forefront of my mind.

Cancun was the perfect remedy. The resort was beautiful, the breeze warm, and the sky a deep and calming shade of blue. The palm trees and lush greenery took me right back to our honeymoon in St. Lucia just six months ago. My heart hurt, but this time in a good way. I was close to some of my happiest memories of Eddie. Having Diana with me filled me with gratitude. I could finally disconnect and relax without the pressures in my life at home.

Over the next days, we spent a lot of time at the pool and on the beach. We enjoyed delicious meals, tropical cocktails, and talked, laughed, and cried together. We even met a few people our age. They were laid back, fun and I realized I could be whoever I wanted to be. No one knew what I had been through or asked me uncomfortable questions.

For a brief time, I was free.

Chapter Eleven

NEW BEGINNINGS

(WITH A FOOT IN THE PAST)

After the personal freedom I felt in Cancun, I came back home knowing I needed to find a place of my own. I desperately wanted space to be alone and breathe. I loved my parents and appreciated all they had done and continued doing for me, but much of the time I felt like I was under a microscope. I craved a home for myself. Somewhere I could break down if I wanted to, watch my wedding video in peace, and feel free to just lie on the floor staring at my ceiling and talking to Eddie. I could go through a bottle of wine without anyone judging me. I needed it. It was time.

I contacted a realtor and started looking at townhomes. My parents didn't think I was ready to leave, but my mind was made up. One evening as I was browsing properties online, my phone rang. It was my mother-in-law, Jeanine.

"Hi Momma B, how are you?"

"Hello my wonderful daughter-in-law."

Her voice was cheerful, which put me instantly at ease. I knew what kind of phone call it would be just by the way she said hello. We spoke often, and needless to say, some of our conversations were really tough. We were there for each other and had broken down on the phone many times before. It always made me feel good to hear that she was having a positive day.

"What's going on?" I asked her.

"I'm worried about Fred. Tommy's moving back to New York, and Walter works all day."

Fred was their dog they rescued two years ago. Shortly after Eddie and I first met, he told me that he couldn't wait for me to meet him. "He looks like a cartoon!" Eddie was right. Fred was the most interesting-looking dog I'd ever seen. A Basset Hound Rottweiler mix, he had a big body, long ears, and stubby legs. His huge paws looked like flippers fanned out at an angle. Within minutes of meeting him, I fell in love with his awkward adorableness. He was gentle, loving, and rarely barked.

Worried, I asked Jeanine, "What's wrong with Fred?"

"Nothing at all. I just feel bad that he's not getting a lot of attention." She paused. "I was thinking . . . would you be interested in taking him?"

Sudden joy infused me—something I hadn't felt in a long time. "Are you serious? Is it okay with Tommy? I would absolutely love to have Fred!"

We continued to discuss it for a while and I could tell she felt really good about her decision. She was already planning a drive in the near future from

California to Chittenango, and would bring Fred along. My relief and joy remained long after that phone call ended. Fred was exactly what I needed: a loving companion to be with me while I took the next step in my life.

I spoke to my parents about it, a little wary since I knew they didn't want a dog in the house. But since they knew I'd be moving out soon and Fred's stay would be temporary, they didn't complain about my keeping him. The next time I drove up to Chittenango to see everyone and to visit Eddie, I came back with Fred.

When Fred and I arrived home, he immediately jumped out of the car and went right to some bushes to urinate. I chuckled, knowing my mom wouldn't be happy about that. A smile lingered on my face as I watched Fred walk around the front yard sampling all the new scents. He had traveled from California to Chittenango, and now to Rockland County. I could only imagine what was going through his head.

No one was home when I unlocked the front door and we walked into the quiet house. I sat on the threshold of the living room and watched Fred explore his new space. Tears rose as I thought of Eddie and wished he was with us. Fred wandered over to me and put his head on my lap. He looked up at me with soulful dark eyes, as if to say, "I know you're sad. I miss him, too. I'm here for you." I scratched under his ears and pulled him close to kiss his head.

"Fred, buddy, it's going to be you and me from here on out. Eddie would be so happy to know that you're with me. I love you so much. Thanks for being here."

Fred at the first golf tournament in 2011

My new companion and I sat for a long time in the peace and quiet. In Fred's presence, I experienced a new kind of comfort, one no person could give me. I felt his love—uncomplicated and unconditional—and knew we were a family.

*   *   *

I renewed my house hunt with vigor, spending all my extra time watching HGTV and looking up townhomes online. I dragged my mom to countless properties for an extra set of eyes. My main concern was finding a place as soon as possible. It was time to be on my own again and finally unpack our belongings. I wanted our home back.

I was looking at several places about three to four times a week and finally found the perfect townhouse that had everything I was looking for. The sale went smoothly, escrow closed fast, and within a month I was moving boxes from storage into my new home. It was a bittersweet feeling. I finally had my own place again but going through boxes of history was extremely difficult. Although it was comforting to have our things again, it was emotionally overwhelming. I was in limbo, stretched between the future and past, moving forward and backward at the same time.

I wanted my new house to be decorated exactly like our apartment, or the closest I could make it. I did have to buy some new furniture, but treasured the pieces left over from our apartment in Louisiana. Eddie's bookshelf, our bed, our joint collection of pictures and knickknacks. Even the simple things brought me comfort, like our wine glasses and cookware. I loved hanging pictures in the bedroom, replicating how they'd been in our apartment. I reverently unpacked the beautiful glass vase Eddie bought me when we decided to move in together. He often filled it with my favorite flowers, stargazer calla lilies, and I vowed to continue the tradition.

While unpacking kitchen boxes, I came across an item I both loved and loathed with equal measure. For all that we had in common, Eddie and I had different tastes in décor. He adored the country-kitchen look, while my tastes ran more toward contemporary and modern trends. To feed his obsession, both my mom and Eddie's mom would send us novelty items with roosters and farm animals on them, like coffee mugs and dish towels.

Shortly after Eddie and I moved in together, we were at the store and he saw a figurine of a rooster. It was a decorative piece that complimented the country-kitchen theme. As I've mentioned before, Eddie became excited over the littlest things. That rooster was most certainly one of them. Despite how ugly the thing was, the joy in his eyes prevented me from rejecting his pleas. Once the rooster came home with us, I hated it even more. It often stared at me, with its beady little eyes mocking me while I was cooking. When Eddie was packing for Afghanistan, I told him the rooster was going with him. He just laughed and assured me that I'd come to love it.

Sitting on the floor in my new kitchen surrounded by boxes, I held that darn rooster and loved it. Just like Eddie said I would.

"You win, Eddie," I whispered. "I love this damn thing."

I hung Eddie's clothes in the bedroom closet, crying the whole time as each piece of clothing brought back a certain memory. I held his shirts close and put on his big, baggy hoodie. After his clothes were hung up, I ran my fingers through the blue and black striped shirt he wore when he proposed, his favorite T-shirt from college with too many holes to count, and his Giants and Yankees jerseys. My most cherished item of Eddie's was his Yankees hat which he wore almost daily. I gently placed it on my head and immediately felt him there.

Some of my friends were concerned when they found out I had Eddie's clothes hanging in the closet. Some thought it was creepy. I didn't care. I didn't care what others thought, and I didn't care if it made me look crazy. It brought me a little bit of comfort and that was something that was rare for me to feel. Having his clothes sharing space with mine made me feel like he was still with me.

I wasn't ready to let go.

*   *   *

In the first year without Eddie, there were so many dates and times that were difficult for me. So many beautiful memories that were now too painful to think about. The day I dreaded most that year was Eddie's birthday. Thinking of my own birthday coming later in June, I already knew I didn't want to do anything. I didn't want to acknowledge it or have any special attention. If I couldn't celebrate Eddie's birthday with him, I didn't want anyone celebrating mine. Eddie would never see the age of twenty-six, and acknowledging my birthday meant I'd be older than him. My life was going on and his wasn't. It was more than unfair—it was an injustice.

When Eddie's birthday arrived in April, I went to visit him. I couldn't imagine being anywhere else. I drove into the cemetery and parked. As I turned to look at his plot, I immediately broke down. I sat there and cried and cried until I finally mustered the energy to head to his grave. I lay down beside him, managing a few words through my tears. Closing my eyes, I felt his arms wrap around me. I felt his lips on my face and his breath against my neck. And I heard his whisper in my ear.

"Please don't cry, my love. I'm here. I'm okay. I'm so sorry you're hurting. I love you so much."

I didn't open my eyes for fear of losing this feeling, for fear of not seeing him next to me. I fantasized about dying in that moment so I could join him. But just like every time before, Eddie saved me, filling my mind with memories of past birthday celebrations. Foremost among them was Eddie's twenty-fourth, when I surprised him at Fort Polk.

At least, I tried to surprise him.

I wanted so badly to be with Eddie on his birthday, but I'd just visited him two weeks prior and had a school commitment that weekend. As his birthday approached, however, I found out the class had been cancelled. I immediately booked my flight to Alexandria but didn't tell Eddie. He was going to be so surprised! When we spoke on the phone, I maintained that I couldn't make it. While hearing his disappointment was hard, I managed to hold the secret inside.

I called a friend of Eddie's, who agreed to pick me up from the airport and not spoil the surprise. I made sure to cover all my tracks. I knew Eddie would find it suspicious when my phone was off during the flight, so I told him that I had to take my phone to Verizon and would call him later on. Everything was going smoothly, right up until the day of my flight. Before boarding, I gave in to temptation and called him just to hear his voice. He asked what I was doing, and I told him I was on my lunch break.

"Are you coming to see me?" he asked excitedly.

"I wish I could, but I have to work."

"I don't know, babe, I think you're coming to see me."

This line of questioning went on for long enough that I realized he'd figured it out. I was so disappointed. Not to mention annoyed. "It was supposed to be a surprise!"

Eddie was overjoyed. "Ah, I'm so excited! I knew it, I just knew it!"

I groaned. "How did you know?"

"Well, Oraby kept telling me that he got me the best birthday present ever, and then mentioned he was going to the airport in Alexandria today to pick up a friend."

My flawless master plan had been brought down by Eddie's excited friend. I should have called a cab! I had been anticipating the surprised look on his face so much that I was crushed now that I wouldn't see it. After getting off the phone, I texted Oraby and told him he no longer needed to pick me up since Eddie knew. I had just enough restraint not to heap blame on his shoulders. As disappointed as I was, I was still going to see Eddie. Surprise or no surprise, I was exactly where I wanted to be.

When I arrived in Alexandria, Eddie's truck was parked right out front. As soon as he saw me he jumped out. Wearing his new suit and a self-satisfied grin, he spread his arms wide as if to say, "Ta-da!" My disappointment immediately vanished and I ran into his arms. When he finally put me down, I asked him why he was wearing a suit.

"I know you were really disappointed that I found out, so I wanted to dress up for you and make you smile."

He couldn't have given me a better answer. Looking in his eyes, I felt like he couldn't possibly make me any happier than I was right then.

The memory of that weekend was so vivid that I completely forgot where I was for a few minutes. For a brief time, I'd been in Louisiana with Eddie. The wind started to blow through the cemetery, and a leaf fell softly on my cheek. My eyes opened and grim reality returned.

I lay beside Eddie for about forty-five minutes before I heard footsteps approaching. Sitting up, I saw it was Finny. He sat down next to me and wrapped his arm around my shoulders.

"Hey Dre, look what I got." He presented me with a bottle of Jack Daniel's and a shot glass. At my expression of distaste, he smiled smugly. He knew that even though I hated whiskey, I was going to take a shot anyway—for Eddie.

Finny poured the shots and handed me one. "Sláinte," we said, raising our glasses.

"Happy birthday, buddy," Finny said, and threw back the shot.

"Happy birthday, Eddie. I know you're laughing at me right now." I tilted my head back and tried to take it in one gulp. Finny laughed at the painful wince on my face. We hung out for a while, rehashing funny stories and sharing our sorrow.

Later that day, we were able to spend some time with Jeanine, who was still in town, and then with Carson's family, the Lindseys. Mrs. Lindsey even baked a birthday cake. As tough as that day was, I was grateful to have so many amazing people in my life. We spent the night drinking, laughing, and crying. But the most important thing was that we were all together, and we were celebrating the life of a man who we all loved and missed tremendously.

Leaving Chittenango was always hard for me. Every time I left, I stopped at the cemetery one last time. And every time without fail, I was overcome with guilt. I wished I could visit him more and for longer periods. I could easily sit with Eddie for hours, thinking about him and the life we should have had. But the hardest was feeling like I was leaving him behind. I was haunted by thoughts of his sad eyes begging me not to leave him. To stay a little while longer.

As crazy as it sounded, the truth was I didn't want to hurt him. I hated that I couldn't visit him every day. A friend once told me that it was better Eddie wasn't closer to me. If he was, the possibility of visiting him every day would consume my life. No doubt I would be there every day, and it would make it harder for me to move forward. She was right, of course, but I didn't want to hear it. I couldn't think about moving on with my life. I was stuck in my fantasy world of Eddie and I being together. I couldn't accept that he was gone, nor did I want to.

As time went on the cemetery became a hangout spot. One weekend, a group of us visited Eddie. We put blankets down by his headstone, set up some beach chairs, opened some beers, and hung out with Eddie. Although it's not true for all cemeteries, this one was peaceful. It was comforting being there.

We were there long enough that everyone was getting hungry. Someone suggested ordering pizza, and Finny concocted the idea of having pizza delivered to us at the cemetery. Feeling like that was pretty morbid—not to mention potentially traumatizing for the delivery driver—I protested. Despite my resistance, I was overruled.

So, that night we hung around Eddie's gravesite drinking beers, sharing stories, and eating pizza that was delivered by an extremely weirded-out delivery boy. Eddie would have loved every second of that night, especially the traumatized delivery boy. In fact, Eddie probably would have demanded we videotape it all.

Other times when groups of us would meet in Chittenango, we'd visit his grave individually. One weekend, Finny had to leave early on the Sunday morning. As he was driving home, he called and told me he left something for me with Eddie. Instantly, I knew what it was. When I arrived at the grave, there was a shot of Jack Daniel's waiting for me. I couldn't help but laugh.

"What an ass," I muttered as I picked up the shot.

Finny, of course, had known I wouldn't be able to refuse.

Eddie received VIP treatment at that cemetery. His plot always had flowers and mementos that had been left for him. The previous winter, I'd come up one weekend after they had a lot of snow. Everything was completely covered. I packed my shovel, knowing it was going to be tough to get to Eddie. As I pulled into the cemetery, however, I couldn't believe what I saw. There was a path to Eddie's grave, and his headstone sat in a wide circle of cleared ground.

The family that took care of the cemetery was amazing—they dug out that path for me and Eddie's frequent visitors. Again, I felt the love radiating from the wonderful town of Chittenango. They knew I needed all the love I could get, and they gave it readily.

Chapter Twelve

(UN)HAPPY ANNIVERSARY

I chose my profession because I love helping people. I was outgoing and confident, and lived by the mantra that strangers were just people I hadn't talked to yet. I loved interacting with others, learning from them, and forming new relationships. But when Eddie died, that bright part of me suffered a near-fatal blow. I never imagined there was such a thing as too much sympathy, too much kindness, too many reminders. Perhaps it depends on the person, but for me, strangers became the enemy. Strangers were synonymous with ripping open my barely-healed scars and bleeding all over myself to assuage their curiosity.

I became a closed-off person. When I moved into my home, I didn't reach out to my neighbors. Being that I live in a townhouse, it was impossible to completely avoid people, but I tried. When meetings inevitably occurred, nerves made me awkward or irascible. Either they already knew what had happened and would bring it up, followed by the all too familiar head tilt, and a sympathetic, "How are you doing?" Or, they would see my wedding rings and ask about my husband.

The only neighbors I felt remotely comfortable around were those directly next to me. They were a friendly couple in their fifties. I often wondered if they knew, but they never pried. I came to find out they did know, but when the dreaded, "How are you?" came, they took my polite reply at face value and respected my space. They didn't bring up Eddie and I was immensely grateful for their intuitive understanding.

I felt relieved. My experiences with most people drove home for me why I held so much resentment toward strangers who invaded my personal life. Rarely did any of these people reach out to me on a human level. To them, I wasn't Andrea, I was a caricature of a widow. One-dimensional and defined by my grief. While they saw their behavior as bestowing acts of kindness, I saw the truth behind their actions. A truth they couldn't admit because they didn't care about me or Eddie. They cared about themselves—about the projected image of the type of person they were. They didn't want to comfort me, they wanted to comfort themselves. Like "Comforting a widow" was a checkbox on a morality list they found satisfaction in crossing me off.

It was a hard lesson in human nature to learn at twenty-five years of age.

*   *   *

After spending the month of July isolated in my new place, I decided to make an effort to get out more. But anxiety continued to plague me. Every time I went somewhere I risked running into people I knew, even though I told myself no one was going to say anything. Yet time and time again, people failed to meet my expectations. While I was overwhelmed with the amount of love and support I received from family, friends, and the community, I was also overwhelmed by the number of ignorant people. I discovered people could be hurtful and selfish. I began to doubt every relationship I had. I questioned their intentions, wondering if they only befriended me because I hated the spotlight, and they wanted to be able to talk about me to others. In a twisted way, I was a minor hometown celebrity. I absolutely detested the attention, but even more so, the effect it had on my psyche.

Eddie was on my mind every day. Everything reminded me of him. No matter what I did, my thoughts involved him. I loved thinking about him. Even though some memories were hard to handle, they were still precious to me. And even though I spent a lot of time thinking about him, it didn't mean I wanted to constantly talk about what had happened.

People thought that because they knew about my situation, they had the right to bring it up whenever and wherever. To preach to me about God's plan, and ask about my stage of grief. Friends and family that had known and loved Eddie had a right to ask those questions. Not random people who didn't truly know me. I didn't want their advice. I didn't want to talk about the intensely personal experience of losing my husband. Maybe that gave me a reputation for being callous, but I didn't care.

The fact that so many people were insensitive to my desire for privacy only compounded my fear of being in public. I'll never understand people's tendency for invasive questions. Grief wasn't a cute new pair of shoes or a hairstyle begging for compliments. It was a hole in the center of my being. While Eddie was always close to my thoughts, I sometimes needed to escape the memories, even if it was just for a few minutes. People clearly didn't understand that.

Every day I experienced a rollercoaster of emotions. It usually started off with the void of depression and numbness, then moved to deep grief. The cycle often ended with anger. Anger was the most exhausting. Above all, it made me feel like a different person, no longer the woman Eddie had fallen in love with. I wanted to be that person again but I didn't know if I could.

I tried filling my life with routines that made me feel good even if it was only for a few moments. I only watched comedic or heartwarming movies and television shows, gravitating in particular toward the effusive positivity of Ellen DeGeneres. I recorded her show every day and watched it in the evenings. Her love for people and faith in mankind was what I needed. I used to be like her—used to see the good in everyone—and I felt like Ellen could help me find the old Andrea again. I worked hard on my outlook by surrounding myself with positive influences.

Trying to find happiness again was hard work.

*   *   *

As the summer came to an end, I finished my last classes and received my Master of Mental Health

Counseling degree. Even after all that hard work, it was still difficult to feel any gratification. I wasn't personally proud of myself but found comfort in knowing that Eddie would be proud. Since I wanted to work in a school, I decided to complete one more internship for my School Counseling Certification. I reached out to my former middle-school guidance counselor, and she happily agreed to take me on as an intern for the semester. I was excited to go back to my old school but nervous as well, especially considering the number of people there who heard about what happened. I was hoping that enough time had passed for the inappropriate comments and questions to stop. I was wrong.

My first morning at the school was prior to the start of the semester, a day designated for staff meetings. I pulled into the crowded parking lot, sitting in my car for a few minutes, and waited for my hands to stop shaking. *You can do this.* I repeated the mantra silently until I felt strong enough to get out. I made it two steps from my car before I was stopped by a former teacher.

"Hi! You're one of the Perez girls, right? Diana?"

"Yes, but I'm Diana's older sister, Andrea."

Comprehension dawned on her face. "Oh yes, Andrea. I know your whole story."

"Know my whole story?" I echoed in shock. This woman knew nothing about me! Before she could speak, I managed to say, "I'm interning here in the guidance department. Nice seeing you." I turned and walked swiftly toward the main building. Anger spiked inside me but I focused on my breathing until it faded. Holding my head high, I entered the school with a smile.

It was great to reconnect with the school's counselor, Kim, and I knew I would enjoy learning from her. I had a lot of plans for groups and was looking forward to working with the kids. After going over the semester's schedule, we went downstairs for a faculty meeting. The principal welcomed the staff and spoke about expectations for the school year. After, Kim and I chatted with some of the other teachers. A few were familiar, having been here when I attended while she introduced me to others I didn't know.

Although I never met her before, one of the teachers knew me because I'd gone to school with her daughter. Right away she cornered me and confessed that she, too, was a young widow, having lost her husband at forty. I stood frozen, staring at her, my tongue glued to the roof of my mouth. The other teachers watched me with varying degrees of sympathy. When the woman finished her life's story, she threw her hands up and said, "Whew! I'm glad we got that over with," like she felt so much better now that my pain had been thoroughly discussed and dismissed.

The emotional knife in my stomach turned, sinking deeper and deeper into my open wound. I knew if I spoke about Eddie I'd break down, and I felt bitter resentment toward this woman for putting me in this position. Finally, Kim sensed my discomfort and politely interrupted the conversation and pulled me away. We went back to her office where I could comfortably be in a secluded area, away from unwanted questions and attention.

Although I hadn't seen Kim in years, I felt comfortable with her. There weren't a lot of people I could say that about, but Kim was different. While I don't think everything happens for a reason, I do strongly believe that certain people were put into my life for a reason. Kim and I were meant to reconnect. During the course of my internship, we were able to help each other. At the time, Kim was dealing with her own difficulties. Her husband of forty years was struggling with Parkinson's disease, and she was forced to watch the love of her life deteriorating before her eyes. Though her husband was still alive, she related to my pain. She was grieving for the husband she once knew. Her husband lost the ability to speak as well as perform simple tasks on his own. She dealt with the helplessness, the struggle with denial, the grief and rage.

Meeting her, you would never have known she was dealing with such hardship. Kim was the bubbliest, most kind-hearted individual I ever met. Her kindness and generosity touched countless lives. Often after the school day was over, we'd have long conversations. We spoke about our husbands, shared funny stories and difficult situations. I was able to express my anger toward others in an environment that was both safe and nurturing.

Despite my rough start, my internship at the middle school was a positive experience. I loved working with the kids, and Kim was a great mentor. The job kept me busy, buffering me slightly from the approach of more *firsts*. I'd gotten through Eddie's birthday, but soon I'd have to face my first wedding anniversary, the return of his unit from Afghanistan, the anniversary of his death, Veteran's Day . . . the list seemed endless. Interning with Kim gave me a small outlet in which I could set aside my heartache and focus on being a professional counselor.

School didn't begin until after Labor Day which was a relief. The holiday marked my wedding anniversary and I knew it would be a hard one. As the date neared, I was once again bombarded with calls, texts, and emails. Everyone was concerned about me, but I soon felt suffocated. Finny called daily, but for the first time I found myself ignoring his calls. I had a feeling he wanted to visit me Labor Day weekend, and although being around him always lifted my spirits, I doubted even he could lift me from the depression that day would bring.

September was quickly approaching and with each day that passed, I felt more and more in a fog. Depression weighed heavily on my body and mind. I spent countless hours imagining how Eddie and I would have celebrated our first anniversary. I fantasized about his smile as we watched our wedding video together and enjoyed our favorite wine. He would dance me around the room, singing loudly and off key. The thoughts made me smile, but their price was pain. The joy we should have felt had been taken away.

One evening, after a long day of work, I came home to a stack of mail. Junk, junk, bills, more junk. Then I came across a card. I stood in my kitchen staring at the envelope in my hand. I knew what it was, but I didn't want to believe it. How could anyone be so insensitive, so utterly cruel? My hands shaking, I broke the seal, hoping against hope that I was wrong. I wasn't. The card read *Happy Anniversary!* Inside, I found a handwritten note, *Congratulations on 1 year!* My stomach knotted painfully and for a moment, I thought I would vomit.

A new type of rage came over me. *One year of what?* I thought. One year of pain and loss? One year of nightmares and loneliness and depression? I couldn't fathom why someone would think it was appropriate to send this to me. When would it stop? When would people learn to leave me alone? I immediately called Diana, who was just as stunned and angry as I was. Her compassion took the edge off my rage. In spite of my grief, I wasn't crazy. This was not okay. No matter how many times I resented the piles of sympathy cards, I never had a problem imagining the good intentions behind them. This was different. Good intentions be damned.

*   *   *

The week of my anniversary, I finally called Finny back. As I expected, he wanted to visit me. I couldn't say no because it wasn't only about what I needed. Finny was in pain too. Our wedding was the last time he saw Eddie and as much as I wanted to be alone, I knew it would be better to be together. Diana would also be in town. I'd have Friday to myself, and Saturday would be spent with those closest to me. Somehow, I'd make it through.

Friday night after a dinner of picking at leftovers, I wandered upstairs to the closet that held my wedding gown. I opened the box and ran my fingers through the beautiful beading and lace. Without a second thought, I pulled out the gown and veil and put them on. The dress still fit perfectly, the satin interior felt luxurious on my bare skin. I moved side to side, smiling at the *swish* of fabric around my legs.

As I walked downstairs, Fred looked at me like I was crazy. He curled up on the other side of the room, dark eyes following my progress to the kitchen.

I pulled a bottle of beer from the refrigerator, cracked it open, and took a big gulp. It was delicious. With one hand holding the bottle and the other lifting the skirts of my gown, I walked into the living room and plopped down on the couch. Fred's uncertain face and hesitant tail-wagging made me laugh. Throwing my bare feet onto the ottoman, I turned on the TV and flipped through channels. I'd already watched my wedding video several times that week, and the part of me that was still rational decided against watching it again.

Too tired and emotionally drained to cry, I sat on the couch in my wedding dress, drinking a cold beer and watching television. *If people could see me now,* I thought to myself with a chuckle. *Instead of a white dress, I'd be wearing a white jacket in a padded room.* I laughed harder at the thought of what Eddie would say. Lost in thoughts, I imagined him gazing at me with a twinkle in his eyes.

I love you, you silly girl.

"I love you, too, Eddie," I whispered aloud. "Happy Anniversary."

On Saturday, Diana came over to hang out and we waited for Finny to arrive. My skin was crawling with the contrasting emotions clashing inside of me. I wanted to sit in a dark room buried under my bedcover. I was nervous to be around more people, afraid that I wouldn't be able to contain my emotions. It wasn't that I didn't feel safe with Finny and Diana, but breaking down in front of anyone was hard for me.

Finally, the doorbell rang and Diana and I went downstairs. Finny greeted me with a bear hug and a smile. Now that he was here, I suddenly couldn't imagine surviving the weekend without him. As we settled in the living room with fresh beers, Finny focused on me with a serious expression.

"Okay, Dre," he began, "I don't want you to feel like you're entertaining this weekend. I'm here to hang out and do whatever you want to do. We can sit around and watch movies all day if that's what you want. We don't need to leave the house. We can order pizza for every meal. If you want to sit in the dark, we can sit in the dark together."

I looked at him and smiled my gratitude, knowing that if I said anything, I'd fall apart. With a few short words, he alleviated the worst of my anxiety. I didn't have to pretend or force any smiles. I could be myself, grief and all.

We spent the day watching TV, drinking, and playing card games. Around six o'clock, my doorbell rang. Panicked, I looked at Diana and asked if she'd invited people over. She shook her head. I couldn't imagine who would show up unannounced. I walked anxiously downstairs and opened the door. As soon as I saw who it was, though, I felt only excitement and relief. It was my sister-in-law, Clare. She gave me a tight hug. Behind us, Diana laughed and said, "Surprise! Don't yell at me but I invited her." Yelling was the furthest thing from my mind. I hugged them both, and my tears were happy ones.

That night as everyone headed to bed, Clare joined me in my room. I was so grateful to have her with me. I was dreading tomorrow. No matter how hard I tried to convince myself it was just another day, it wasn't. It was a day that had meant so much to Eddie and me. A day I'd cherish forever. A day I should have been able to celebrate each year with him.

Clare and I fell asleep talking. For once, I slept hard and deeply, without nightmares. When I woke up Sunday morning, Clare was gone and I had a knot in my stomach. Voices filtered upward from the kitchen, pots and glasses clinking as people made breakfast. I didn't move, not wanting to face anyone yet. I rolled over and stared at the empty space on my bed, running my hand over the smooth sheets where Eddie should have been. Closing my eyes, I summoned his memory.

Good morning, wife! Happy Anniversary. Come closer—you're not close enough.

I could feel his arms pulling me tightly against him. Taking a deep breath, I smelled his cologne and savored the moment. It passed all too soon, and reality settled back in. I turned my back on the emptiness and stared at the wall until tears blurred my vision.

A few minutes later, there was a soft knock on my bedroom door. I managed to call out, "Come in," and everyone entered carrying my breakfast on a tray. I had absolutely no appetite, but smiled at how sweet it was of them to make me breakfast in bed. I forced myself to take a couple of bites, then concentrated on my cup of coffee.

I wanted to stay in bed all day but after finishing my coffee, I managed to get myself up. I showered and dressed, then put on my bravest face and went downstairs. It was a relaxing day filled with junk food, movies, and laughs. My parents stopped by for a while to check on me and give me their love, and a few other friends came and went.

Time passed minute by minute, and midnight came and went. It was September 5, 2011. Surrounded by the love of my friends and family, I made it through my first wedding anniversary without my husband.

Chapter Thirteen

OVERCOMING THE FIRSTS

Firsts are always hard. First time you fall off a bike, first day of school, first date, first time you leave home. Grief is no different, though harder. I'd been told many times that in the case of losing someone, after the *firsts* it gets a little easier. I held on to that hope, desperately wanting all the firsts to be over with so I could have some kind of relief.

Some days the pain was unbearable. I missed him so much it physically hurt. Other days I found a sort of twisted peace with my depression—welcomed it, even—as it helped numb my broken heart. I focused as much as I could on work, took whatever comfort I could from Fred, and put one foot in front of the other. Time, indifferent to my suffering, moved forward. Half of me followed, and half of me stayed rooted in the past.

Around the end of September, I received a letter in the mail from Fort Polk inviting me to attend the homecoming ceremony for Eddie's unit. I couldn't imagine anything more tortuous. While I greatly appreciated Fort Polk's attempt to keep me involved and part of the military family, there was no way I could stand there watching while the soldiers were reunited with their families. I was sincerely happy that the men of Eddie's unit would finally be able to leave that horrible nightmare of a place and come home. But I was envious and angry as well. It wasn't fair or right that Eddie wouldn't get to experience the same welcoming arms as these soldiers.

With growing certainty, I knew I couldn't be around when the unit came home. I had to get away. Finny would be gone on vacation, but Ben and I decided to visit Carson in California. It was a trip we all needed. Two days after Ben and I booked our flights, however, I received a letter in the mail from Eddie's high school. He was going to be inducted into the Chittenango Athletic Hall of Fame. I read the letter over and over, a huge smile on my face. Eddie would have been ecstatic about this. We'd often shared memories of playing sports in high school. The experiences were some of our fondest ones from our youths. I could easily envision Eddie running around holding his plaque up high with pride. This would have meant so much to him.

Upon reading the letter a final time, I noticed the date of his induction was the day before Ben and I were supposed to fly to California. Although anxiety spiked through me at the thought of receiving attention, I knew I had to go for Eddie's sake. After talking to Ben, we changed our flights so we'd be leaving from Syracuse, and I did my best to prepare for another round in the spotlight.

When I drove to Chittenango, I stopped on my way into town to buy flowers. I always visited Eddie first. It was early evening when I made the drive and now the night was dark and quiet. A breeze blew gently through the cemetery as I laid my flowers down next to Eddie. I kissed a single rose and placed it on his tombstone.

"I know you're smiling big tonight, my love."

After spending some time with Eddie, I drove to the Lindseys' house where friends and family were gathering. I loved being in that house and always felt a sense of comfort there. Unfortunately, this time I was greeted with news that made my stomach clench. Tomorrow's game and ceremony were going to be televised. There would be reporters at the field, as well as a camera crew. Panic gripped me. Nausea rose in my throat. Mrs. Lindsey saw the look of terror on my face and gave me a big hug. Everyone present knew how much I hated all the attention I'd been getting over the last year.

Finny put his arm around me. "It's okay, Dre. We'll be there with you the whole time. Just think how excited Eddie is right now."

His words helped, and a vision of Eddie's smiling face softened my anxiety.

The next evening, we caravanned to the high school. Tommy and Clare wore their old high school colors, their faces radiating excitement. As we pulled up to the school, I noticed the packed parking lot and news trucks close to the entrance. I instantly felt a lump in my throat. *One foot in front of the other,* I told myself. *You can do this for Eddie.*

The stadium was overflowing with people wearing red and black school colors and cheering for their team. As we entered, the principal spotted us and directed us to a large tent that was set up for Eddie's family and friends. I was happy to see his aunts, uncles, and cousins all there showing support. There was a beautiful picture of Eddie on a plaque showcasing his accomplishments. Being surrounded by people who loved him eased some of my tension.

My reprieve only lasted a few short minutes before a reporter spotted me. With an anticipatory smile on her face, she cornered me where I stood beside Finny.

"You must be Edward's widow!"

I glanced at Finny, and we shared a knowing look. *Did she really just say that?*

"My name is Andrea," I said flatly as she reached out to shake my hand.

"I'm Marie from Channel 12 News. I'd love to get an interview with you."

"Well, um . . ."

My hands shook, my breathing went shallow, and my thoughts bounced between terror and a stubborn vision of Eddie's smiling face. *Can I do this? For Eddie?* I opened my mouth and what came out surprised me as much as Finny.

"Okay."

The reporter flashed a blinding grin. "Great! Let me just grab the camera crew."

"Camera crew?" I bleated. "Sorry, no way. I don't want to be on camera. Finny here is great with interviews. He's the person you want on camera."

Always happy to speak on Eddie's behalf, Finny nodded in agreement.

The reporter's smile dimmed a little. "But sweetie, you look great!"

Ignoring the patronizing comment, I said rigidly, "I don't feel comfortable being in front of a camera. If you'd like an interview, you can speak with Finny, Eddie's best friend."

No longer smiling, the reporter glared at me. Her fake, I'm-so-nice act was gone. "Listen, I was told that I would get an interview with you. Interviewing his friends is great, but we really want to bring it home with you."

I stiffened in surprise and annoyance. "I have no idea who told you I'd do an on-camera interview, but I never agreed to that."

Finny moved forward protectively. "You heard her, she doesn't want to do an interview. If you'd like to speak with me, I would be happy to do it."

"Fine!" she snapped. "I also heard his siblings are here. Can you show me who his brother is?"

"Sure thing," Finny said quickly. "Follow me. I'll take you to him."

As they walked away, he glanced back with a sly smile. I watched as he led the reporter on a wild goose chase around the tent, always in a direction opposite from Tommy. The reporter grew more frustrated with every passing minute. Finny was undeterred, and led her right out of the tent into the bleachers while Tommy stayed perfectly anonymous nearby.

Twenty minutes later, Finny returned with a smirk on his face. Laughing, I thanked him for being such a good actor and an even better friend.

As halftime and the ceremony grew nearer, the principal explained to me what to expect. "We'd be honored if you accepted the award on Eddie's behalf."

My heart started racing. I turned to Tommy and Clare, who stood nearby. "Will you both go up with me? I can't walk up there alone." They immediately agreed, and I breathed a sigh of relief.

At the start of the ceremony, the principal introduced the athletes and their accomplishments, then gave a short speech about Eddie and the positive influence he had on people, both on and off the field. Afterwards, the school's superintendent, Mr. Schiedo took to the stage. The words filtered in and out of my mind, though some sentences stuck fast.

"….displayed courage in everything he did… A true leader… captain of the varsity football and baseball teams his senior year… named in several all-league and all-region teams… team player, a great role model… always positive and never complained… work ethic and personality outshined his athletic prowess."

As the powerful speech drew to a close, I straightened my spine and blinked back tears.

"Bolen was the type of kid who loved life, who always did the right thing. Unfortunately, his life ended too soon. In addition to presenting the scholarship for Eddie, the athletic department has decided to memorialize his jersey, number forty-four. To ensure Eddie's spirit lives on at our school, his jersey will be presented each year to a player who exemplifies courage, selflessness, and leadership."

He then called me up to accept the award for Eddie. With the roar of the crowd in my ears and Clare and Tommy by my side, I took the award. Instead of seeing hundreds of faces staring at me, I saw instead Eddie's radiant smile.

*   *   *

I flew to California the following morning. It was the perfect escape, and I was thrilled to spend some time with Ben and Carson. Just being with them—and out of New York—lifted the thick pall of depression from me. We spent a few days enjoying laid back barbecues, the beach, and touring Carson's favorite places in San Diego.

On October 12, I woke up with the now-familiar knot in my stomach. Another first had come—the day Eddie would have returned home from Afghanistan. Today would bring so much joy to other families but was an emotional slap in the face for me. Deep down there was still a part of me that was in denial. A part of me that believed they'd made a mistake and that Eddie would still be returning home.

My relief that his unit was home, the men safe, was matched by an equally potent longing for a moment that could never be. I wanted to be in that gym when they came marching in. I wanted to run up to Eddie and lose myself in his arms. As my scars split open once more, I was so grateful not to be home. I was with amazing friends in a beautiful place.

But no matter how far I ran, I couldn't escape the pain.

With the return of Eddie's unit, I only had one more first remaining—the one-year anniversary of his death. I fell back into my normal routine, hiding my misery beneath my work ethic. School, internship, home, school, internship, home. I went through the days on autopilot, afraid of confronting the truth. Almost an entire year had passed. It felt like time was playing tricks on me again. There was no way a year had gone by, not when it still felt so new to me.

In one of the first sympathy cards I received, someone had written a famous quote inside. "When you're going through hell, keep going." It was my only choice then and my only choice now, but I needed to know this "hell" would end someday. I clung as hard as I could to the idea that it would get better, that this was the worst of it. I needed the pain to become less consuming. I needed to feel some sense of peace. My life was filled with so many incredible people who I loved dearly, but I still felt so angry and alone. My heart ached for Eddie every day, and living stretched between the past and the future was slowly killing me.

November 10, 2011 fell on a Thursday. I took Thursday and Friday off, knowing I wouldn't be able to function at work. Wednesday evening, Diana and I drove to Chittenango to be with those who made me feel like Eddie was still with me. Alerts for calls and texts streamed into my phone as people sent their love. I had a tremendous amount of support from so many people.

In Chittenango, the typical crew gathered. We spent time at the cemetery with Eddie, both in groups and individually. My private visits with Eddie were the times I valued the most. Just Eddie and me, as if we were together again. I spent hours upon hours crying over him. Sometimes I'd talk to him, sharing thoughts and feelings, and other times I'd retell funny memories and imagine him laughing with me. When I closed my eyes, I could feel him with me. I could feel him sitting next to me, pulling me closer and closer. But when my eyes opened again, I was alone.

The brisk air made cold rivers of my tears. "I miss you terribly every single day. I love you always and forever."

I kissed my hand and placed it on the beautifully sketched image of Eddie's face. When I walked back over to my friends, Finny already had his arms open for me. Gathered at the Lindseys' house that night, we ate, drank, laughed, and cried together. Everyone's pain was apparent, but being together truly helped. It was amazing how alive Eddie felt when we were all together. It was as if he was in the room with us, laughing at the jokes and sharing each toast.

My phone continued to buzz intermittently with notifications. Among the usual well-wishes were some that were definitely going to be added to my ever-increasing journal list of dumb statements. But the jaw-dropping moments didn't stop there. On Facebook, one of Eddie's ex-girlfriends had posted on his wall, confessing her everlasting love for him and sharing how in love they'd been. I felt it was an extremely inappropriate message. The day had been difficult enough for me without having to read that. And that was not the only one. My friends were supportive and just as upset as I was. To spare us all more anguish, I turned off my phone.

With my friends we made many toasts to Eddie, often accompanied by hilarious memories.

"Remember that time when Eddie ran out of the shower with a small hand towel covering his junk and he asked, 'Hey, where are all the big boy towels?'"

"Remember when I texted Eddie the word 'touché' and he came bursting through my door thinking I insulted him by calling him a 'tushie' because he pronounced it wrong in his head?"

"Remember when we threw his Yankee hat up on the roof of that bar? He snuck away a half-hour later, hunted down a ladder, and retrieved it. He came back in wearing his hat with the most self-satisfied smile we'd ever seen."

At the end of each story, everyone laughed and raised their glasses.

When the clock struck midnight, conflicting emotions overwhelmed me. Sadness that it had been a year. Relief that the dreaded *firsts* were finally over. When I left the next day, it was with pain in my heart. It was always hard to leave Eddie, but this time felt different. The thought of causing him pain made me sick.

"I'll be back soon, my love," I swore. "Always and forever."

*   *   *

Midway through interning at the middle school, we had a crisis meeting which consisted of the counselors, teachers, and the principal. The purpose was to discuss, brainstorm, and create a plan if there was a crisis in the building. This included determining where a safe place would be to bring the kids, who to call, et cetera. Several scenarios were presented, including a fire in the building, a gunman, a natural disaster, and finally, a bomb.

I was enjoying the meeting, listening avidly to different strategies and comments from the staff. That was until the instructor played a video of what to do if there was a bomb in the building. Right away, I had an uneasy feeling. I ignored it, trying to stay focused on work and leave my mind out of

Afghanistan. Easier said than done, especially when the instructor referenced the war in Afghanistan.

A ton of broken-hearted pressure invaded my chest, squeezing my lungs and compressing my breath. The demonstration video started off okay, with a discussion of the roles of the people involved. Then it showed the principal walking through the halls. An explosion went off right next to him and he flew into the opposite wall. My body, my breath, my heart . . . all of me froze except my mind.

My mind was with Eddie. I flashed back to all the time I'd spent obsessing over his death, imagining ad nauseam the detonation of the IED. Between my imagination and research, I formed a vivid picture of what happened. I knew what was said before the explosion, and what expression Eddie wore. I knew what the explosion sounded like, how the air smelled, and could hear the aftermath of shouting and gunfire. And I knew what had happened to my husband's beautiful body.

Trapped in the horror in my own mind, my hands grasped the arms of my chair until my knuckles turned white. I wanted to bolt from the room but was afraid of standing. I wasn't sure my knees would hold me. There was a very good chance I'd collapse and break down. I didn't want the attention or to make a scene.

From the corner of my eye, I could see my supervisor trying to make eye contact with me. She knew how difficult this was for me to watch. But I didn't look at her. The sympathy in her eyes would fracture my perilous control. Others glanced my way, but I avoided all eye contact. Was it in my head? Were they really looking at me, waiting for me to freak out? I wondered if I was finally losing my mind.

I kept hearing the explosion, over and over, and seeing the looks on the soldiers' faces as they watched Eddie's life being taken away. I could see our friend Sean clearly as he ran through the firefight just to collect Eddie's dog tags. I could hear screaming, shouting, crying. My body shook and I held my chair tighter, my back ramrod straight and my face bloodless.

When the video finally ended, there was a brief discussion before we were excused. The second people started rising from their chairs, I got out of there. My head down to hide my face, I fetched my purse from the office and made a beeline for my car. I drove to a corner park far from the school where no one would see me. Then I lost it.

Someone was screaming—it took minutes to realize it was me. I cried so loud and so hard that I could barely breathe. My heart pounded so fast I felt like it was going to come through my chest. The harder I tried to slow down my breathing, the more labored it became. There was only one person I wanted and needed to talk to. I had to talk to Sean.

It took me fifteen minutes to calm down enough to make the call. It went to voicemail. What was I thinking? Sean was at work—of course he wasn't going to pick up. But I had to talk to him. I called a couple more times, and he finally answered.

"Hey, Dre-Dre. Sorry, I was in a meeting but I stepped out." I think he knew I wasn't doing well. Why else would I call him four times in a row in the middle of the day? Normally when he didn't answer I'd just leave a message.

I opened my mouth but nothing came out. All I could stammer through my tears was, "Sean."

"What's going on, Dre?"

I could hear the concern and pain in his voice. He knew I was crying, but did not know what had triggered my grief. Eventually, I managed to tell him about the video and what had happened to me while watching it.

"I know soldiers get flashbacks, Sean, but I wasn't even there! It felt so real. Like I was actually there. I saw everything."

"Aww Dre, I'm so sorry. I can't even imagine you having to see that."

Through sobs, I stammered, "Part of me is happy you were there with Eddie at the end, but the other part of me hates that you saw that. I know it's hard for you. I hate that you have to go through this. I feel like I can't breathe. When is this going to get easier?"

"It is really hard," he admitted quietly. "I don't know when it's going to get easier. I wish I could block out those memories. I love you, Dre. I'm so sorry."

We spoke for a few more minutes before hanging up. I still felt like crap, but at least my mind was my own again. I was in that parking lot for a half-hour before I was composed enough to go back in. I found a napkin in my glove box and wiped away the tears, then put in some eye drops to get rid of the redness. I took some deep breaths and the tremor in my hands finally eased. "I love you, Eddie, I love you Eddie, I love you Eddie," I whispered, over and over until the affirmation gave me the courage to finish my workday. I walked back into the school with my head held high, like I was a strong, confident woman. A lie, but a necessary one. There simply was no alternative.

That was one of my worst breakdowns, but definitely not my last.

Chapter Fourteen

MOVING FORWARD

A year and a half is a long time to live lost in depression and pain, waking up every morning wishing you hadn't. The thought of finding happiness again, experiencing a loving relationship with another man, stirred up a tremendous amount of emotions. Guilt being foremost, and the hardest one to swallow. Even the idea of kissing another man, being intimate with someone else, or developing feelings triggered guilt.

My future was supposed to have been with Eddie, and now all I had was the unknown. Moving on without him was the most difficult reality to accept. But I did know I had to learn to deal with the pain and not let it control me. I had to overcome it and allow the possibility of opening myself up to happiness. Ultimately, I knew happiness was what Eddie wanted for me.

I just didn't know how the hell I was supposed to find it.

I was utterly lonely, but couldn't wrap my head around dating again. In my mind and heart, I was still married. How could I even think about being with another man? As time passed, though, every so often my mind would wander to thoughts of what it would be like to date. It seemed so foreign to me. The only man I wanted was the one I could no longer be with.

On a Friday evening at the end of March, I picked up the phone and called my sister. I haltingly explained how I was feeling—the intense loneliness coupled with fear of intimacy. With Diana's encouragement, I decided that what I needed was to meet and spend time with more people. That strategy would allow me to hit two birds with one stone—get over my fear of strangers asking questions and reignite my love for new experiences.

That evening, I took a risk that unbeknownst to me, would once again alter the course of my life. While on the phone with Diana, I thought about different people who had come into my life and who I wanted to spend more time with. One person in particular kept coming to the forefront of my mind. His name was Arash. He was a friend from the gym that I'd met years ago and he always kept in touch. Not a lot, but here and there through the years. We would refer to each other as "gym Bffs" because we would talk the whole time while working out. Actually, he usually did most of the talking. I enjoyed his funny, animated stories and his positivity. After moving back home, I started going to my old gym again. Arash was one of the few people I felt comfortable sharing details about my life with. The main thing, I knew, was that he saw *me*. Not the widow, just Andrea.

When I told Diana about my tentative idea to hang out with Arash outside the gym, she encouraged me to go for it. "If he puts you in a good mood and makes you smile, then do it." She was right. He did put me in a good mood, and he also knew my situation. I wouldn't have to worry about him thinking that hanging out together would be romantic.

After I got off the phone with Diana, I texted Arash. He was thrilled that I reached out, and we made plans for dinner the following evening. We decided on sushi because it was a favorite for both of us. Impulsively, I invited him to my place for a glass of wine beforehand and he agreed, offering to bring the wine.

I woke up Saturday morning excited about the night to come. Whenever I saw Arash at the gym, he was always upbeat, talkative, and easygoing. He was the ideal person to help me become the sociable person I once was. I was convinced that the secret to finding myself again was surrounding myself with positive, fun people. He fit the bill perfectly.

Late that afternoon, I stared at the clothes hanging in my closet and hated them all. For the first time since texting him, I felt a flutter of nerves. I subconsciously recognized that it stemmed from a desire to look pretty, which made no sense. This wasn't a date. This was simply catching up with a friend. I berated myself for my thoughts, then dismissed them as a result of being out of practice. Wanting to look nice didn't mean anything, right? I told myself *no,* while a little voice in the back of my mind whispered, *maybe.*

Eventually deciding on jeans, a black top, and my favorite boots, I applied a little makeup and gave myself a final once-over in the mirror. Natural, casual, approachable. I looked good, confident, and felt more like my old self than I had in months. I could do this. If I couldn't be the old Andrea again, I could be a new version. Maybe even a better one.

When Arash arrived, he greeted me with a smile and a quick kiss on the cheek, then offered me a bottle of wine. I laughed when I saw the label. At his questioning look, I told him it happened to be my favorite.

He smiled. "Mine, too. Looks like we both have good taste."

I gave him a quick tour of the townhouse, then we made our way to the kitchen. As I pulled out a couple of wine glasses and opened the bottle, Arash studied a painting of Eddie which hung on the wall.

"This is amazing," he said softly.

I looked at Eddie's smiling face. "Thanks, I think it is, too." I handed Arash a glass of wine. "We've been saying we should hang out forever. I'm so glad we finally made plans."

He grinned. "Me too! You look great, by the way."

"Th . . . thanks," I stammered. Shockingly, I felt my cheeks grow warm. I could tell by the awareness in Arash's eyes that he noticed my reaction, but was relieved when he didn't say anything.

Settling with our wine at the kitchen table, we chatted about what was going on in our lives. I felt comfortable enough to talk a little about Eddie, and he shared that he'd recently broken up with his girlfriend. The news didn't surprise me. The last few times I'd seen him at the gym he told me things weren't going well. After hearing more about the issues and drama in their relationship, I told him that clearly he made the right choice. He agreed wholeheartedly.

Difficult topics out of the way, our conversation progressed. We talked about traveling, friends and family, and shared laughs about various experiences at the gym.

"Remember that time you fainted?" he asked with a twinkle in his eyes.

I groaned, covering my red face with my hands.

A couple of years prior, I decided to give blood at a local firehouse. I'd given blood many times before and never had any problems. That occasion, however, was a different story. The nurse drawing my blood was new, and she must have stuck me twenty times before she found a vein. There was little I could do but watch in horror. When she finally succeeded, I was so ready for the experience to be over that I pumped my fist as fast as I could to encourage blood flow.

I felt fine that night and went to the gym the next morning. Seeing Arash behind the counter, I stopped to say hello. Seconds later my vision started tunneling inward and white noise filled my ears. I tried to speak, to tell him I think I needed to sit down, but it was too late. In a lobby full of people, I hit the floor.

I was only out for a few seconds, and came to with Arash hovering above me. He and another employee helped me to an office and offered me water and granola bars. Mortified that I'd passed out in public, I told them it must be because of giving blood. The other employee cheekily suggested it was because of Arash's breath. We all chuckled.

Recalling the mingled embarrassment and humor of that day, we laughed again. We kept talking and laughing until we realized it was close to nine o'clock. Luckily, the sushi restaurant was right down the road from my place. Once there, we ordered saki and rolls, and continued where we left off.

Arash did most of the talking, but that was fine by me. He was an animated storyteller, and I spent the entire dinner smiling and laughing. Lost in our own world, it took us a while to realize the wait staff was eyeing us impatiently. Besides us, only one other table was occupied. When they eventually left, we decided to leave before we were kicked out.

The drive back to my place was brief, and as we pulled into the driveway, I had the stunning realization that I didn't want the night to end. Moreover, it was obvious that Arash felt the same way. Without further thought, I invited him inside. We opened another bottle of wine and kept talking, migrating from the kitchen to the living room couch.

I couldn't remember the last time I had so much fun, felt so at ease. Grief, I learned well, has a funny way of messing with time. The last year and a half felt simultaneously like the blink of an eye and a lifetime all in one. And now here I was—anchored in the present. Wearing no masks or filters to hide my true self. I felt a glimmer of peace.

Not until we were both yawning did we look at a clock. It was five-thirty in the morning! We talked through the entire night though it felt like mere hours had passed. I could see my own shock reflected on

Arash's face. As our eyes locked, it seemed like we were both realizing the undeniable spark between us. Staring at him, I saw someone I'd known for years, a steady, friendly presence in my life. And for the first time, I also saw the man. The handsome, funny, kind man. A string of emotions came over me and I realized I wanted to kiss him.

So I did. I was shocked at how quickly I acted upon my desire to kiss him. Time didn't allow me to overthink it. As he kissed me back, I felt the passion he'd been holding on to. Nothing felt more natural in that moment.

By seven o'clock in the morning, the adrenaline from the night started to wear off. We fell asleep side by side on the couch, my head on his shoulder and his arm around me. Two hours later, the sun roused us. For a few minutes, I felt the same peace I had last night. As I made coffee, we laughed and talked like what had happened between us was perfectly normal. That waking up together was no big deal.

Then it hit me. It was a big deal. A really, really big deal. I'd kissed another man.

There was guilt, then more guilt for feeling the first guilt. Embarrassment for my boldness in kissing Arash. Relief that I still possessed the capacity for passion which I thought was lost to me. I wondered, too, if he would want to see me again, or if he planned on running out the door and never coming back. Did I even want to see him again? How is it possible to be smiling and freaking out at the same time?

My stomach churned with mingled anxiety and excitement. This was a huge step for me and something I didn't think would ever happen again.

The need to confess to someone was overwhelming. I felt like I was about to erupt.

Whatever thoughts Arash had, he kept to himself. But I knew deep down that he was just as surprised at the turn of events as I was. I also knew that if I hadn't made the first move, he wouldn't have kissed me. He respected my situation and wouldn't have wanted to make me feel uncomfortable. That knowledge kept the worst of my panic at bay. He wasn't taking advantage. He was a friend I'd known for years. And after our marathon of conversation last night, he was a friend I knew extremely well. His beliefs, his fears, his favorite movies and music. Family, morality, thoughts on life and death. We covered it all.

When I walked him to the door that morning, I had mixed feelings. Part of me didn't want him to go while another part was dying for him to leave so I could call my sister.

We lingered in my doorway. Feeling suddenly awkward, I cleared my throat. My face, I knew, was bright red. "Well, I didn't see that coming," I told him.

He laughed. "Neither did I. But I had a really great time."

I thanked him again for dinner. He gave me a gentle, sweet kiss goodbye, and left.

The second the door closed, I ran to my phone and called Diana. Immediately after I told her, I had to pull the phone away from my ear because she was cheering so loudly. When she calmed down, she told me how proud of me she was and that she knew how hard it was for me to step out of my comfort zone. After hanging up, I called my friend Jenna. When she answered, I blurted, "I know it's April Fool's Day, but

I have something to tell you and it's not a joke. Are you home?"

When I got to her house, I sat down with her and explained what had happened. As she listened, her smile grew wider and wider.

"Andrea, this is huge."

"I know, but I'm freaking out. A part of me feels like I cheated on Eddie. But it was also really fun to be with someone again. I'm dying to know what's going on in Arash's head. Does he want to see me again or was it just a one-night thing?"

Jenna listened while I ranted and raved, and finally grabbed my hands. "Try not to beat yourself up. This is a good thing. You deserve to be happy and have fun." Her smile turned teasing. "I think your phone just rang."

Sure enough, it had. I saw a missed call and voicemail from Arash. Turning wide eyes on Jenna, I said, "I guess my questions are about to be answered."

As I listened to the voicemail, a smile came over my face. "Hey Andrea, it's Arash, I hope you're doing okay. I'm exhausted and going to take a nap in a little bit. I just wanted to tell you that I had a really, really great time last night. You're a great girl and I really enjoyed your company. If you're up for it, I'd like to see you again."

He sounded normal, maybe a little nervous. Knowing he had as much fun as I did last night felt really good. Though I still didn't feel like I was ready to date or be in a relationship, the prospect was no longer as terrifying.

When I returned home, I worked up the courage to call him back. I was a little relieved when it went to voicemail. But then nerves took over. I rambled for at least a minute about how much fun I had, how glad I was that we hung out, and that he was the first guy I'd kissed since Eddie. On that awkward note, I hung up and covered my face with my hands. My heart was racing, and I was convinced that I'd just sent him running.

Then he called back. I immediately apologized for my idiotic voicemail.

He laughed. "You sounded adorable. When can I see you again?"

Chapter Fifteen

BABY STEPS

Arash and I weren't dating. We weren't in any sort of relationship. Hanging out with him was fun, freeing, and without complications. He was a perfect distraction from my daily pain. That's what I told myself, at least. But as we continued to see each other, sometimes several times a week, my conviction started to waver. I found myself thinking about him and daydreaming about spending time together. My sister told me I was smitten. I scoffed at her maintaining that it wasn't serious.

I was in outright denial.

Being the perceptive person he was, Arash never called me on it. He knew this was new territory for me, just as scary as it was exciting. When the truth battered too hard at the door of my denial, I reinforced the boundaries between us. I told him that I wasn't ready to be in a relationship, that I still loved my husband. Pictures of Eddie were all over my house—in my bedroom, my living room. His clothes were still in my closet.

I must have sounded like a basket-case more than once, but for some reason Arash didn't run screaming. He listened to my rants, told me he understood and respected my feelings. He accepted me just as I was, all the different parts of me. Grieving wife, widow, scared woman, and—when I let myself—someone who very much enjoyed spending time with him.

*   *   *

On one particular evening, all my fears and doubts surfaced. I'd spent the last few days with my sister who was then living in Kansas City, and despite the great trip, I was dealing with the uncomfortable feeling of how much I missed Arash. Admitting to myself that I was developing feelings for him was impossible. I chalked it up to the teenage-like experience of having a harmless crush. Whatever I needed to tell myself to minimize what was happening, I did.

As soon as I returned from my trip, Arash came to my house for dinner and a movie. The sight of him brought a genuine smile to my face. But soon, I was going to have to accept that we were more than just friends. When I went to grab a couple of wine glasses, it triggered feelings of guilt. My gaze snagged on the ones that were Eddie's and my favorites, leaving flashbacks of the fun, romantic evenings we shared. The world slowed down as a weight settled in my stomach. I immediately try to brush away the feeling while reaching past the glasses for two others. "I deserve to be happy" I chanted to myself. Walking to the table where Arash was waiting, I hid my growing disquiet behind a smile.

"So, I wanted to ask you something," I began hesitantly. "Have you told anyone about us hanging out?"

"Not really," he answered as he poured wine. "My friend Joe knows because I talk to him often. Why?"

Swallowing the knot in my throat, I sat down. I didn't know how to say what I wanted to without it coming off as rude, so I just went for it. "I don't want to sound like a jerk, but I'd appreciate it if you didn't tell people about us. It's not that I'm embarrassed by you by any means, and I know you know that. But I feel like I've been under a microscope and people are watching my every move. Everywhere I go, people know what's going on in my life. It's weird and invasive. I want my life to be private, and this is still new and scary for me."

Once again, Arash surprised me with his compassion and acceptance. If anything, my honesty was refreshing for him. Perhaps it took away the pressure of trying to guess my motives. Or maybe me being upfront about what I was and wasn't comfortable with prevented the misunderstandings and unnecessary drama he'd struggled with in his prior relationship. Whatever his thoughts were, he still wasn't running. In fact, it was quite the opposite.

Later that same night, I turned from the kitchen sink and caught Arash watching me. I recognized something in his eyes I hadn't seen in a long, long time. He was looking at me the way a man looks at a woman he wants and adores. But more than that, it was the way a man looks at a woman he respects. No one had looked at me that way since Eddie. Until now. I wasn't remotely prepared for what I saw in Arash's eyes.

On the one hand, it felt good—affirming. On the other?

I was petrified of what it meant.

*   *   *

The next moment of truth came not long after. Arash was over and decided to join me for a walk with Fred. As we headed out through the complex, he reached for my hand. In public and in broad daylight. I was stunned and had no idea how to react. I only knew I didn't want my nosy neighbors to see us holding hands like a couple. We were not a couple. We were just hanging out. I held his hand for a brief moment, then let go to pet Fred.

I felt like a juvenile and a fraud. Here I was spending time with someone I liked—who obviously liked me—and I was too scared to accept the growing intimacy between us. Too scared to even hold his hand. Lost in my dark thoughts, I wondered if I would feel this way forever. *Will I always be this paranoid and crazy? How long with Arash put up this?* The thought of him walking away was sobering. I didn't want him to.

The following day, I called Diana and unloaded all my fears. As usual, she was able to talk me off the ledge by reminding me that what I was feeling was perfectly normal.

"This is all new for you, Dre. Just take it one step at a time. Keep being honest with him, and don't do anything that's outside your comfort zone. You're going to have good days and bad days. If it's too much hanging out with Arash, then take a step back. Listen to your heart."

Unfortunately, my heart was the most confused part of me. It was still broken, the wounds just beginning to scar. I missed Eddie. I *love* Eddie. There simply wasn't space in my heart for anyone else. Even a funny, considerate, intelligent man who treated me with the utmost respect, who I loved being around, and made me feel special and *seen*. The truth—however good I was at denying it—was that I wasn't ready to admit that my heart was already involved. As it was starting to slowly heal, it was being filled and renewed.

*   *   *

Arash came to my house often, so I finally suggested going to his place. He was surprised. "Are you sure about that? I live on the corner of a busy street, and a lot of people could see you."

His words were a wake-up call to say the least. For the first time I saw the burden I was placing on him with my condition of not letting people know about us. I thought about all the pictures of Eddie in my place. Unless he was a robot, he had to be at least a little bothered by them. I saw my unwillingness to hold his hand in public, my obsession with people judging me, and wondered again why on earth he was sticking around. His understanding and diligence in respecting my wishes was incredible. *He* was incredible.

"Yes, I'm sure."

*   *   *

On a Friday evening in early May, Arash invited me out to drinks with some of his friends at a local restaurant. There was no expectation in his voice. If anything, he probably figured I'd refuse, as the restaurant was a place frequented by people I knew. But day by day, little by little, my comfort zone had grown.

It was a nerve-wracking night. As anticipated, many people approached me to say hello. I used Arash and his coworkers as an excuse not to chat with anyone long and to avoid the awkward questions and condolences. But the night was also necessary— Arash finally witnessed firsthand the reason for my social anxiety.

*   *   *

"We have a lot of fun together and I enjoy talking to him . . . "

Sitting across from me on the couch, Jenna's brows lifted. "I sense a 'but' coming."

"But, I'm still not ready to date."

She gave me a look of mingled sympathy and determination. "Call it what you want, Dre, but the reality is you're dating."

Diana had said the same thing to me, but I'd brushed it off. This time, however, the words sunk in.

"Holy shit, you're right. I'm dating? That sounds so weird."

Jenna laughed. "It isn't weird. It's awesome."

From the panicked knot in my stomach, I wasn't convinced. "I'm scared, Jenna. About people finding out, judging me, or thinking it means I don't love Eddie. I don't want people talking about me or asking about me. What if they see me holding hands with another man? What would they say?"

Jenna grabbed my hand. "You need to stop worrying about what everyone else thinks. People will talk, but you can't let that control your life. If anyone has anything negative to say about you moving on and dating, then they're just selfish. They don't know what you've been through, and they don't know anything about your relationship with Eddie. The people who love you the most are happy for you. We're thrilled you're taking this huge step and trying to be happy again. We all know how in love you and Eddie were. You two were our inspiration to find true love for ourselves. Don't let people ruin your chances of finding happiness again."

Her heartfelt words made me realize the biggest source of my fear.

"I don't want to hurt anyone. It feels like that's what I'm doing."

Jenna looked at me like I was crazy. "Do you hear yourself? You need to stop worrying about everyone else and focus on yourself. You need to do what will make you happy."

Deep down, I knew she was right. I did need to care less about what strangers thought of me. But what about those who'd known and loved Eddie? What about Finny, Carson, and Ben? The Lindseys and Eddie's family? His parents, brother, sister . . . No matter how sound Jenna's advice was, I dreaded them finding out. I didn't want to hurt them.

*   *   *

Every small step I took into the future brought healing. One of the most rewarding moments was when I finally told Clare I was dating. Since she was studying abroad at the time, I wrote her a long email and hit Send before I could change my mind.

Twenty-four hours later, Eddie's sister—*my* sister—replied. As I read her words, another wound in my heart sealed closed.

Dre,

Look at you go! I'm so happy for you! And don't be silly, it's not weird for me at all. It sounds like you have a really open relationship with this guy which is amazing given the circumstances. I'm glad to know you can tell him when something doesn't feel quite right. From what you told me, it also sounds like he's really into you—but then again, how could he not be?

I definitely understand that this is a huge step for you, but I couldn't be happier that you feel like you can talk to me about this. You're my sister and I love you! I think you're right not to look into things too much. Hang out with him, have fun, be honest, and you'll be just fine.

I can't wait to see you again! You're in pursuit of happiness and attacking it in all the right ways. I am happy for you!"

Pursuit of happiness, indeed.

Chapter Sixteen

NEW FREEDOM

On a beautiful Saturday in May, Arash and I decided to spend the day in Central Park. As we walked through the city, Arash grabbed my hand. My fingers automatically curled around his. Whether it was due to being anonymous in a city of millions, or the gorgeous spring day, I felt comfortable being affectionate with him in public.

At Arash's suggestion, we stopped at a hotdog cart outside the entrance to the park. He was so excited, like he'd waited all his life for a Central Park hotdog. His energy was contagious, and we each ordered. Arash made sure to tell the woman no onions on his.

He smirked at me. "I plan on kissing her today."

The woman smiled. "Are you enjoying this beautiful day with your wife?"

He laughed. "We're not married, just dating. But yes, I am."

To my embarrassment, the woman glanced at my wedding rings. Though she looked away and served us without further mention of it, my stomach sank. She probably thought I was cheating on my husband. We paid for our hotdogs and walked toward the park entrance. I stuffed my guilt and embarrassment deep inside and focused on enjoying the day instead of overthinking things.

Not until Sunday evening, when I was home alone, did I confront my conflicting feelings. I wasn't ready to take off my rings. They felt as much a part of me as my limbs. But after Clare's supportive email, I started to realize I needed to tell more of my friends about Arash. So many people had stood by my side for the last year and a half. Not telling them I was dating someone felt like as much of a betrayal as I feared telling them would be.

Despite the support I already received, I worried constantly about people not being able to understand that I needed to move forward with my life. On some level, I knew they wouldn't turn their backs or cut me out of their lives, but the fear of their judgment was enormous. Thankfully, Jenna and Clare's words stayed with me, giving me just enough hope that those who loved me wanted to see me happy above all.

I decided to start with Christine. One of my oldest friends, she'd been a confidant since before my relationship with Eddie. She watched me fall in love, and supported me through the happy times as much as the difficult ones. Our ritual of bar hopping and girl-talk had fallen off in the tumult of the last year, but I was feeling stronger now. Not the old Andrea, but the new one. Bolstered by our ten-plus years of friendship, I made plans a few weekends after to meet Christine at a Yankee game.

I wore my Jeter jersey and Eddie's hat even though it was clearly too big. But the hat was one of Eddie's most treasured belongings, and I hoped it would bring me luck. Christine and I met outside the stadium, then grabbed drinks and found our seats. We made small talk while inside my chest, my heart raced at the prospect of telling her I was dating. By the middle of the third inning, I couldn't hold it in anymore.

"There's something I've been wanting to tell you, but I didn't want to do it over the phone."

She looked puzzled. "You know you can tell me anything. What's up?"

I took a deep breath. "I'm dating."

A huge smile bloomed on her face. She leapt from her seat and began jumping up and down, cheering like someone had just hit a home run. People around us stared and laughed, as red-faced with embarrassment, I yanked her back down to her seat.

The second she sat down, questions came pouring out of her mouth. "Who is it? Is it someone I know? Where did you meet? How long have you been dating? How many guys are you dating?"

I laughed after hearing her last question. "I'm having a hard enough time wrapping my head around dating one person, let alone multiple guys."

"This is so amazing," gushed Christine. "We all know how much you love Eddie, but I think it's wonderful that you're dating and trying to move on."

I blinked back tears of relief and heartache. "It's been really difficult for me to wrap my head around it.

I keep worrying about what everyone will say, but even more so, I can't help feeling like I'm hurting Eddie. I know that sounds silly, but I can't help it."

Christine hugged me tightly. "Eddie would be heartbroken to see you hurting. I have no doubt that he's happy knowing you're looking to the future. If anything, it reminds him exactly why he loved you so much. You're becoming the strong, courageous woman he married."

I couldn't speak, so I just hugged her. My heart and mind were a mess, but I was overwhelmed with gratitude for her words. Words that were both painful and true. I felt like I could see myself as the woman my friends and family cherished and loved. I only wished that becoming myself again didn't mean leaving Eddie behind.

When I told Arash about Christine's reaction, he couldn't hide his relief. Again, it struck me how stressful our unique situation was for him. Moved by his ceaseless support, I apologized for putting him through all the craziness. He shook his head, a small smile on his face.

"Listen Dre, I'm crazy about you. I'm not giving up. At least at the end of the day I can say I tried. That's all I can do. I'm in it for the long haul."

Looking into Arash's warm hazel eyes, I had an epiphany that shook me to my core. Wherever Eddie was, near or far, and however complicated his feelings might be, he would approve.

*   *   *

In June, Arash invited me to spend the weekend with him in Vermont. He co-owned a townhouse with another family in West Dover, a small town near

Mt. Snow. I felt another shift inside and I happily agreed to go. It was another step forward, scary and exciting at the same time.

Thursday night as I was packing, my gaze caught on my wedding rings. I'd taken them off a few times in the past for short periods, but always put them back on. Now, as I stared at them, I felt torn. How could I possibly go away for the weekend with another man and wear my wedding rings? It didn't feel right.

"Baby steps," I said out loud. "It's just a weekend. Take them off for the weekend. It will mean so much to him. He's been so unbelievably patient."

The pep talk helped. Early the following morning, as Arash pulled into my driveway, I looked once more at my rings. Then I pulled them off, squeezing them tightly in my hand.

"I hope you understand Eddie," I whispered. "I'm really trying to be happy. I love you."

I placed the rings gently in my jewelry box, grabbed my bag, and headed downstairs. Opening the front door and seeing Arash's smile confirmed for me that I was doing the right thing. He loaded my bag in the trunk as I settled in the passenger seat. My heart pounded hard as I waited for him to join me. "There's something I want to show you," I said, holding up my left hand.

He stared at my bare ring finger in shock. "Wow," he breathed. "Are you sure?"

I nodded. "I'm sure."

With a grin teasing his lips, he started the car.

* * *

Even though it rained most of the weekend, we had a great time. It was freeing in a new way for both of us. A weight had been lifted from Arash's shoulders, and I was able to embrace simply being myself. A woman on a weekend getaway with an incredible man.

We toured the small town and took in the breathtaking scenery. The mountains stretched for miles covered in lush green trees. We zip-lined and raced carts down an alpine slide. The bond between us grew steadily with each passing moment. It had been so long since I felt carefree and fully present in my life.

And it was because of Arash.

Little by little over the following weeks, I shared my news with the people I loved. Every occasion was marked by anxiety. Not once was it easy. But I was constantly blown away by the encouragement and support I received.

My lingering hesitance to fully go public with my relationship was taxing for both me and Arash. I walked an emotional tightrope of honoring my need for baby steps while also trying to assure him that it wasn't because I was embarrassed of him. It was hard for him, and it was hard for me. Arash still didn't give up.

*   *   *

Before long, I knew I had to tell Finny. I didn't want him to hear it from anyone else. He'd been a pillar of strength during the hardest time of my life. I owed him so much, not the least of which was honesty.

I drove up to Chittenango on a Friday evening to visit Eddie and to see everyone. The usual crew gathered for a typical, fun night of drinks and laughs.

Every time I worked up the nerve to talk to Finny, something stopped me. There were too many people around, I didn't want to kill the mood, the timing wasn't right . . . the list continued. My chance finally came the following day, when Finny and I carpooled to the Lindseys' house.

I was a wreck of anxiety, my hands clammy and shaking on the steering wheel. My stomach rolled with nausea. Knowing it would only get worse the longer I waited to tell him, I blurted it out, "Finny, there's something I want to tell you."

Concern etched his face. "What's up, Dre?"

The knot in my stomach tightened further. With a sideward glance, I said, "I'm dating someone."

Another look showed me his thoughtful expression. "You are?"

"Y-yes," I stammered, "and I was terrified to tell you."

"What? Why?" he asked in surprise. "Dre, that's great news. You know Eddie would want you to be happy."

I released the breath I'd been holding, relief unraveling the knot inside. Finny asked a few questions which I answered honestly.

Just as I knew he would, Finny made one request. "You know I need to meet him, right?"

*   *   *

Every day I tried to push myself more and more. Each friend I told, each hug and word of encouragement gave me the confidence to take the next step. After a few months, I decided it was time to tell my parents. It wasn't that I believed they'd disown me or anything so dramatic, but I also knew how much my struggles had weighed on them. They were protective before Eddie, and those instincts had only grown after his death. I knew I'd be in for a barrage of questions. I finally felt ready to handle them.

On a sunny Saturday in July, I joined my parents for dinner on their back deck. After a relaxing meal, I sat back and took a deep breath.

"There's something I want to tell you."

"What? Are you moving?" asked my dad.

"No, I'm not moving." My heart raced as they stared at me, waiting for me to speak. Finally, I answered, "I'm dating someone."

My mom smiled, her eyes misting with happy tears.

Unsurprisingly, my dad's first question was, "Who is he?"

I told them how I felt, how it had just happened. As my dad kept pressing for Arash's identity, my mom told me how thrilled she was to hear the news. I knew at least part of her happiness was relief. Seeing me so depressed for so long had been really hard on her.

"Who is he?" my dad asked for the sixth time.

I finally cut him some slack. "Well, you actually know him. He goes to our gym. His name is Arash, and he used to be a trainer there."

My dad frowned. "I think I know that guy." Then, to my ever-lasting relief, he grinned. "I'm happy for you, Andrea."

Phew.

*   *   *

After dinner, I drove to Arash's house to tell him what I'd just done. At first he was worried, but after hearing their supportive reaction the relief was written all over his face.

"When can I meet them?" he asked. "I know your dad and I met him a while back at the gym, but I want to shake his hand."

My first thought was, *Crap*. I didn't feel ready for that. My mom's overprotective behavior manifested as worry for my well-being, while my dad took his Papa-bear instincts to the next level. I wanted to shield Arash from what could potentially end up to be a third-degree grilling from my concerned father.

Looking at the man in front of me, however, I realized how self-centered my thoughts were. Arash rarely asked anything of me. He was consistently respectful of my boundaries. And moreover, his true desire to meet my parents was written clearly on his face.

Despite my reservations, I couldn't say no.

A few days later, Arash joined my parents and me for dinner. I showed up first, so nervous I immediately opened a bottle of wine—much to my mother's amusement. Taking my glass outside, I mentally prepared myself for the worst-case scenario which would no doubt end with Arash running from the house.

I needn't have worried. Arash was his usual charming, confident self. He shook my dad's hand like he told me he wanted, chatting easily with him about people they knew in common. When he discussed family with my mom, she gave me a look of unreserved approval. Dinner went smoothly and the conversation flowed.

Another step forward.

Chapter Seventeen

FOLLOWING MY HEART

As time passed, I felt increasingly comfortable being in public with Arash. Being with him was easy and fun. We spent time at the beach, went into the city, enjoyed barbecues, and hung out with his friends. In July, the first big test as a couple came in the form of a four-day trip organized by my friends Katie and Cody. They were friends of Eddie's from high school, and I'd developed close bonds with them. They rented a house in Ocean City, Maryland, and invited the entire Chittenango crew.

Finny would be there, as well as Ben and a few other friends. Everyone was excited to meet Arash. My former anxiety about going public with our relationship was mostly gone, but I was still nervous. It wasn't judgment that worried me, but the typical thoughts of a woman introducing the man she's dating. *Will it be awkward when I don't use the "B" word? What if Arash is uncomfortable? What if people talk about*

Eddie? Years of anxious thinking had left their mark on me. I knew in my gut that everyone would get along great, but my old, anxiety-ridden self continued to make it difficult to move forward and accept my newfound happiness. Accepting another man into my life also meant carrying around a burden of guilt and fear that I was hurting Eddie.

When we arrived in Ocean City, it was around midday. Everyone was already at the beach. I received numerous texts from Finny on the drive, and knew he wanted to be the first one to meet Arash. I was right. As Arash and I walked toward the beach, Finny found us before anyone else. I gave him a big hug, then introduced him to Arash. They shook hands and exchanged greetings. No disasters or drama beyond Finny laughing at how nervous I was. *Take that, anxiety!*

Finny led us to the rest of the group, and I introduced Arash to everyone else with positive results. They were all happy to meet him and extremely welcoming. We enjoyed a great afternoon on the beach, and the fun continued back at the house. Arash fit in seamlessly with my friends, who treated him like they'd known him forever.

Sitting back and enjoying the sight of everyone together, I knew it was time to stop fearing the "B" word: boyfriend. Arash and I were clearly in a relationship. It had been months since we discussed making our relationship monogamous. I almost laughed when he first brought it up by asking if I was dating anyone else. Back then, my commitment was pretty simple—I barely had the capacity to date one man, let alone several. Now, however, it was much more than that. I didn't *want* to see anyone else. As much as I could be, I was committed.

A few days after we returned from Ocean City, Arash and I went out with two of my girlfriends from high school, Laura and Gina. Like all my other friends, they were dying to meet him. As we pulled up to the restaurant, I felt excitement fluttering inside. Another step forward was happening, and I couldn't wait for Arash's reaction.

When Laura and Gina arrived, I introduced Arash as my boyfriend. Turns out the "B" word wasn't nearly as scary as I'd thought. Especially given his reaction of shock and pleasure. After, as the girls walked ahead of us toward the restaurant, Arash gave me a tight hug and a kiss. The smile on his face beamed with gratitude.

I was a lucky woman.

*   *   *

The next morning, Arash and I were lying in bed relaxing before starting our day. He was being his usual goofy self, telling me grandiose stories, exaggerated for my amusement. Laughing at the ending of his most recent story, I laid my head on his chest.

"Dre?"

"Yeah?"

"I love you."

He said it with unmistakable certainty. He loved me.

I froze, my thoughts chaotic. I cared about him deeply, but felt totally overwhelmed. I wasn't ready for the "L" word. Not yet. Enough time passed without me responding that shame and panic swamped me. I did the only thing I could think to do—looked at him, smiled, and gave him a kiss. I felt like an idiot.

Later on that day, Arash pulled me aside. From the look on his face, I knew I hadn't succeeded in hiding my discomfort. I wasn't uneasy about his feelings toward me, I was annoyed with myself. I wanted to be on the same page as him, but worried that I might not be able to get there because of my damaged heart.

He sat me down and said, "I want to talk to you about earlier."

Oh boy, here we go.

"I knew when I told you how I felt, you'd have that reaction; that you'd look like a deer in headlights. I understand you're not there yet, but that doesn't mean I need to hide how I feel about you."

The bubble of tension inside me deflated, hope filling its place. I threw my arms around him and squeezed him tight, thanking the universe for delivering me someone willing to put up with me.

"Thank you for being so understanding," I whispered. "I really care about you, Arash. A lot."

Even if they weren't the words he longed to hear, I sensed that for now, they were enough.

*   *   *

I knew that in order to keep moving forward, I had to make changes and take risks. But I kept to my conviction of moving at my own pace. "Baby steps" was my mantra.

As summer progressed, I looked at my house with new eyes. Pictures of Eddie were everywhere. It was a shrine. Arash was staying over more and more, sleeping in my bedroom with a favorite picture of

Eddie on my nightstand. The old me, lost in memories and my mind, would have never considered the impact of the photo on anyone else. But the new me had grown enough to consider the burden on Arash. Although he never said anything, I realized how hard it must be for him to love a woman who seemed obviously devoted to someone else.

Over the past year, I'd known that friends and family felt concerned about the abundance of photographs spread throughout my home. They knew, as well as I did, that I would have freaked out if anyone had mentioned them. Defensiveness and anger were my worst—and sometimes most prevalent—coping mechanisms. I was sure there were people who, in my shoes, wouldn't have wanted the daily reminder of their loss. But I wasn't them. I was me, and I had to do things in my own time. My timeline often changed. Some days I felt ready to take a big step, and other days it felt like I took three steps back. Some people wanted to tell me it was time for me to move on, but no one knows the depth of pain a grieving person is going through. Each person's grief is unique, and every timeline is different.

Gradually, I began to take down photos and place them in an album, one or two at a time. Each occasion, guilt shared space in my heart with determination. Knowing it had to be done didn't make it easy. The photograph I was most hesitant to remove was our wedding picture. Hung in the entryway when arriving at the main floor, it was the first thing you saw walking upstairs. Arash had never said anything about it, but putting myself in his shoes, I realized there was no way I'd have been able to deal with that. As I stared at my beautiful wedding photo,

I wondered again why Arash was putting up with me. Was I really worth it? His level of patience and understanding was superhuman.

But even superhumans have their breaking points.

*   *   *

In early August, Arash and I went out with a bunch of friends in Hoboken, New Jersey. It was a beautiful day out and a great crowd. We went to a trendy restaurant with an incredible rooftop bar. It was a large open space, filled with tables on the side, a large bar, and upbeat music. It was still light out when we arrived, allowing us to people-watch as individuals strolled through the city below us. Throughout the night, we drank, danced, and laughed. It was the most fun I'd had in a while. Fuzzy from a little too much alcohol and high on life, I told Arash I loved him. It wasn't so much a confession of deep love. It was more like a drunken, "you're the best person I know and I love you." Definitely not the circumstances in which he'd want me to say those three little words.

I woke up the next morning and didn't think much of it. The memory was vague and the fun alone was intoxicating. I really didn't think it was a big deal. However, Arash was quiet and distant. At breakfast, I asked him what was bothering him.

He was silent for a few minutes, mulling over his words. Finally, he let me see how angry he was. "I don't even know what to say to you," he began.

"Just tell me," I pressed. "What's wrong?"

"You need constant approval from everyone around you. I feel like I'll always be second and never be good enough. You can tell your friends, even my friends, that you love them, but when you accidentally said it to me while you were drunk, all I could think of was you wishing you could take it back."

I sat back, stunned but also grateful for his honesty. So grateful. I could feel a boundary I wasn't aware existed coming down. Depending on my answer, we would either move forward from this, or not. All the times he'd been patient, compassionate, and strong floated before my eyes. He withstood more than most men would. Any man, for that matter. The constant reminders of Eddie, the lingering anxiety and depression, my hesitance to commit . . . He wasn't superhuman—his reaction told me that much. But he was pretty damn close.

With every ounce of conviction I possessed, I told him the truth, "I'm so sorry I'm making you feel this way. This is all new to me. Some days I feel like a basket-case, and other days I feel like I've grown so much I don't even recognize myself. I know this hasn't been easy for you, but you need to know that since the first night we hung out, I've felt the possibility of happiness again. I wish I could tell you how long it will take me to give you what you need, but I just don't know."

Arash didn't stay over that night, and I didn't blame him.

It was a moment of truth in our relationship. Had he had enough? Would our conversation build deeper intimacy or drive a wedge between us? I hoped for the former and feared the latter.

My answer came the following night in the form of a beautiful man arriving at my front door. Arash gave me a hug and a lingering kiss. Whatever the future held, for now, we were walking toward it together.

*   *   *

Not every baby step I took was one I could take alone. This fact soon became glaringly apparent. I spent hours each day berating myself for being unable to tell Arash I loved him. I couldn't find a solution. I knew I was crazy about him. He was an amazing man. He made me feel special and loved, but I was powerless over my thoughts that I was still in love with Eddie. *How can I love Arash when I still love my husband?* I grew haunted, uncertain of myself, and finally reached my own breaking point.

During a phone call with my roommate from college, Marykay, I found myself dumping all of my contradictory feelings on her. She listened to me ramble on about Arash and Eddie, and I finally admitted the most painful truth of all.

"I don't feel about him the same way I feel about Eddie." Even as the words came out of my mouth, I flinched at how harsh they sounded.

Marykay wasn't horrified or surprised. "You're thinking about it the wrong way," she explained. "Why should you feel the same way about Arash? He's a completely different person. It's okay to feel differently. You *should* feel differently. And more than that, Dre, it makes perfect sense that you would love them both differently."

Absorbing her words, I felt like heavy clouds were parting in my mind. I realized the answer was so obvious. I'd put so much pressure on myself to explain what I was feeling for Arash. But by comparing the two relationships, and defending my feelings of love for Eddie and Arash, I'd done all three of us a disservice. I'd always carry the pain of losing Eddie. Nothing would ever change that but I'd come so far. The pain didn't control me anymore. I wasn't going to continue torturing myself and accept unnecessary feelings of guilt. Instead, I was going to treasure it, remember the past, and live for the future. I knew Eddie would want me to be happy, and Arash made me happy.

I had to let go of my guilt and stop denying the obvious truth.

The Sunday morning after that phone call, I woke up in Arash's arms. As the sun shone through my window bathing us in clarity, I looked at his smiling, sleepy face. And I told him the truth in my heart.

"I love you, Arash."

His eyes widened, his smile spreading. "I love you too, Dre."

Andrea and Arash in 2013.

Chapter Eighteen

REALITY CHECK

Halloween was just around the corner, and I received a call from Finny inviting Arash and I to spend it in Chittenango. The crew had plans to dress up in full costumes, rent a limo, and spend the evening hopping around to different vineyards in the area. Although Finny was convinced Arash would be fine hanging out in Eddie's hometown with his old friends, I wasn't so sure. I said I couldn't promise anything, but that I'd ask.

When I told Arash, I made sure to let him know I completely understood if he didn't want to go. A part of me was even hoping he'd say no, if he wasn't comfortable. But once again, he donned his superhero cape and agreed. Despite the nagging thought in the back of my mind that he was concealing his discomfort, I knew I didn't have a choice but to take him at his word.

199

Halloween night went off without a hitch. Most of the people joining us had already met Arash in Ocean City, and those who hadn't were just as welcoming. We had an incredible time in the ostentatious pink limo Finny had rented. The vineyards we visited all got a kick out of our costumes. Finny and his girlfriend dressed up as Danny and Sandy from *Grease*. There was Ron Burgundy, Big Bird, the cast from *Jersey Shore*, the guys from *Brokeback Mountain*, a functioning twister board, and I was the girl from the funny Sun Drop soda commercials. However, my favorite costume was Arash's. After picking on my dad for his attire during his youth, Arash dressed up as a younger version of my dad, complete with seventies afro hair, short baseball shorts and high socks. Although I kept a concerned eye on Arash, looking for signs that he was uncomfortable, I didn't see any. Once more, my worry had been pointless.

The next morning I got up early and went to visit Eddie. I told him about Arash and begged him to be happy for me. I knew he was, and that he didn't want to see me in pain, but a shadow of guilt still remained in my heart. I stayed for a long time, talking to him about my life, and how far I'd come. I told him about school and my career plans, and updated him on our families. Whenever I was with him, I felt such peace. It was always difficult to leave. That day was particularly bittersweet because I was leaving him to return to Arash.

When we left town later that afternoon, our route went past the cemetery. Arash asked if it was where Eddie was buried. I nodded, wanting so badly to stop but not knowing how to ask. My ritual of saying goodbye on the way home was so ingrained that I couldn't imagine not stopping. Arash, of course, was accommodating, and let me run to Eddie's gravesite. I obviously didn't ask him to join me and he respectfully waited in the car while I gave Eddie a quick goodbye.

Walking back to the car, I felt better. Lighter. It wasn't until I got inside and looked over at Arash that I realized how awkward it must have been for him. I had no idea what to say. I couldn't apologize, because that didn't feel right, but I nevertheless felt guilty. The discomfort I was watching for all night was now right in front of me. And it was my fault.

*   *   *

I'd spent so much time holding tight onto Eddie and only wanting him that as I fell more and more in love with Arash, my sense of peace also grew. While the two shared similar characteristics, like a great sense of humor, chivalry, and kindness, they were completely different people. And I was happy about that. I knew I couldn't have another Eddie, just as I knew there was only one Arash. I had a new man in my life. Someone who brought completely different feelings and experiences to the table. But I learned that being different didn't mean less incredible.

While I reveled in my newfound freedom and serenity, Arash slowly began to grow somewhat distant. I didn't know if I was overthinking things, or if the so-called "honeymoon phase" was simply over. We still saw each other often, but it was apparent that something was missing. The intimacy we built with our open, honest communication was fading.

The day after Christmas, he came over. When I saw his face, I knew something heartbreaking was coming. And it was. Unbeknownst to me this was only the beginning.

The ache in my heart told me I could lose him forever.

"There's something that's been bothering me," he began. "Something I've been thinking a lot about the past six weeks. I feel like I'm constantly under pressure. Whenever I walk by the painting of Eddie, I tell him that I'm doing my best, that I'm trying. But it doesn't feel like I can ever do enough—*be* enough. It's bothering me so much that I'm becoming angry. I feel like I'm constantly in his shadow, that I'll never be number one in your heart."

As much as I was grateful for his honesty, the words hurt. They confirmed that my instincts about him distancing himself from me had been correct. It felt like we'd come to a fork in our relationship. We'd begun moving in separate directions and I wasn't paying attention. While I'd been falling more in love, he'd been moving farther and farther away.

I wish Arash had said something earlier before his feelings had escalated to this point. I tried to reassure him that I was putting him first, but deep down I don't know if I even believed my own words. Arash said he didn't want to be distant, and promised he'd be more open with me. He wasn't ready to give up and I was immediately relieved. He wasn't letting go. He was willing to work on getting our relationship back onto solid ground.

I didn't think either of us knew how hard that would be.

*   *   *

We spent New Year's Eve in Times Square, having scored free tickets from one of Arash's friends. Around midnight, we ventured from the bar where we were celebrating and out into the insane crowd. We'd both been drinking, and the intense press of people and screaming chaos was overwhelming. We managed to see the ball drop, then struggled through the throngs back to the bar.

We were both irritated, but for different reasons. I was disappointed that our first New Year's together hadn't lived up to my expectations. The reason for Arash's simmering anger? I had no clue, but was bound and determined to find out.

Back at my place the following morning, I confronted him.

"We need to talk about last night."

He sunk into a kitchen chair and put his head in his hands. "The resentment we talked about is still there. I've been trying so hard to let go of it, but I can't. I'm afraid that if I don't take some time to figure this out, I'll wind up hurting you emotionally."

Numbness consumed my body. "Are you breaking up with me?"

"I don't know, Dre. I don't want to, but I can't shake the feeling that I'll never be number one in your life. There are pictures of you and me hanging right next to pictures of you and Eddie. I want to be the man in your life. The *only* man."

"You *are* the only man in my life," I argued. "You helped me to lower my walls and fall in love. You've made me happy again!"

Arash just shook his head, his pained eyes meeting mine. "I want to believe you, I do. But I don't feel it. I love you so much, and you're the greatest thing that's ever happened to me. You are my princess. I used to do things for you because I wanted to take care of you, but I've noticed myself holding back. That's not fair to you. I know you'll be an amazing mother and wife someday, and I want that future with you. But another part of me fears that even after that, I still won't be number one. I need to take some time to figure this out."

Time. Always time. It had been both a blessing and a curse in my life. Crawling when I wanted it to fly, racing by when I wanted it to stall. After all the pain I'd escaped and grown past, at the end of the day I was still powerless over time.

On New Year's Day, Arash and I cried together and hugged each other tightly. He walked away, only to return to hug me once more. Then he left. The door closed softly behind him. Time, just like it had more than two years ago, ignored my heart's plea to rewind.

*   *   *

Arash had never asked me to do anything I wasn't ready for. Even when I did take huge steps, he would always ask for reassurance that I was okay with the change. Never once did he request that a photo be taken down or any of Eddie's things put away. Everything I did was on my own terms and when I felt ready. His understanding and selflessness had always seemed superhuman to me, even too good to be true. Now I knew that underneath his heroic exterior was a real man. A complex, emotional person just like me, who struggled with doubt and fear. While this revelation deepened my love for him, it seemed like I'd come to the realization too late.

Alone in my house, my heart cracked and broke all over again. I was hurt that he played the role of "perfect" for so long, obviously afraid to drive me away with demands. I was also angry that he hadn't been honest sooner. A large part of my pain was knowing that I'd been hurting him. Arash had said he felt like I would never put him first. I was so hyper-focused on moving forward at my own pace that I missed the signs of his unhappiness.

He was gone. Taking time to think about himself and us. As he wondered about the future, I walked into the past. Upstairs in my bedroom, I opened my closet and ran my fingers along Eddie's clothes. I took out one shirt at a time, examining each piece while memories played in my mind. I remembered when they were worn, fun memories and sad ones. I remembered conversations, events, difficult times, and especially the laughter that was a hallmark of our relationship.

I held certain items close to my chest, closing my eyes to feel Eddie with me. I saw his smile, and heard him say, "It's okay baby, you can let go. I'll love you always and forever."

Tears came as I separated the clothes I wanted to give to his family and friends. The rest would be stored away carefully in bins. As I stared at my half-empty closet, a feeling I had not expected came over me. My tears slowed and stopped. For the first time in over two years, I felt as if a huge weight had been lifted from my shoulders. The weight I put there. Now I could breathe again. It was time. I found out how to finally let go.

I put so much pressure on myself to keep Eddie's memory alive that it had held me back from living my own life. I couldn't live in the past any longer. Eddie would always be a big part of my life, and I would always love him. But now I accepted that I deserved to have a future. Letting go didn't mean I'd stop loving him or thinking about him. It meant cherishing my memories, but allowing myself to make new ones.

As I closed the closet door, I remembered a quote by Joseph Campbell: *"We must be willing to let go of the life we had planned so as to have the life that's waiting for us."*

I had a new life waiting for me.

Chapter Nineteen

SIGNS AND SECOND CHANCES

The weeks following Arash's decision were hard. I'd finally come to peace with my past and here I was, heartbroken again. At least this was familiar ground. I knew how to put one foot in front of the other, surviving by simply going through the motions. There were many times I wanted to reach out but held back, wanting to respect his wish for time and space.

I was depressed and lonely, but I took a page out of my past and forced myself to accept social invitations. Depression was a slippery slope for me, and this time I was committed to fighting it. As much as I missed Arash, I needed to keep moving forward. But no matter how many times I had fun with friends, at the end of the night I was alone again.

On a Sunday evening about two weeks after our split, I was lying in bed trying to turn my head off so I could sleep. My phone buzzed on the nightstand. I rolled over to see a text message from Arash.

I miss you.

My heart dropped, tears filling my eyes. I wrote back, *I miss you, too.*

It wasn't much, but I'd learned to appreciate even the smallest steps of growth.

*   *   *

Monday morning, I went to the gym before work. When I saw Arash already there, my heart started racing. *Does he regret texting me? Is he going to talk to me?* I tried to put the thoughts aside, focusing on my workout. As I finished, however, Arash approached me. He looked sad and concerned as he told me it seemed like I'd lost weight.

It was true—I hadn't had much of an appetite recently, a familiar symptom of my depression. Despite his obvious concern, I was angry, too. I wanted to ask why he cared, or tell him it was none of his business.

Biting back my sarcasm, I lied. "I'm fine. How are you?"

He told me about his weekend spent snowboarding in Vermont. As usual, I was soon laughing at his story. The interaction was so familiar that for a second, I forgot that we weren't together anymore. When I remembered, it was like a slap in the face. I couldn't pretend to be friends with him. Talking to him, laughing with him, only reminded me of what we'd lost.

I cut the conversation short and all but fled the gym. I decided to run some errands so I drove to a nearby bank to use the ATM. As I pulled into a parking spot, my phone rang. It was Arash. My thoughts ping-ponged madly between options. Answer. Don't Answer. *Answer!*

"Hello?"

"Hey, Dre. It was really nice talking to you this morning." He paused to take a deep breath. "I've been doing a lot of thinking and want to talk."

My heart leapt with hope even as my mind cautioned me against it. But regardless of whether he was calling to break up for good or reconcile, I needed to know.

"I'm actually just down the road. I can come over in a few, if that's okay?"

"Perfect. See you soon."

When I arrived, he greeted me with a tight hug. *So far, so good,* I thought as we walked into his kitchen and sat down. Hands clenched in my lap, I waited for him to speak.

"I miss you like crazy, Dre. For a long time, I really thought I could handle everything—I *was* handling it. Trust me, if I'd known it would all hit me this hard I would have tried to tell you sooner. It was more of a feeling that kept building and building inside me. The feeling that I'll never be first in your life. Before I knew it, it was controlling me."

Still not knowing what direction the conversation was going, I took the risk of telling him what was in my heart. "I know I haven't made this easy for you, Arash. I've come so far, and a huge part of my growth is because of you. And you're right, I've had a hard time letting go of Eddie. I didn't put you first, and I'm sorry. But I want you to know that something's happened, something's changed. After you left that day, I packed away Eddie's clothes."

His brows lifted. "I find that hard to believe."

"Well, it's true. And do you know what happened when I was done? I felt lighter. Free. And I realized that was the last major step for me in letting go. I'll never stop loving Eddie, and he'll always be a part of me. I know you respect that. But now I feel like I finally have peace. I've been holding on to him so tight, terrified of hurting him. I know that sounds ridiculous but I couldn't bear the thought. A part of me has always known he only wants me to be happy, and I am, now that I'm with you. Everyone, including you, have been so supportive, but it was ME who needed to feel like I could give one hundred percent of myself to someone else. I finally feel confident that I can."

As I sat back, my cards all on the table, Arash's eyes shone with gratitude. And, unless it was wishful thinking, I also saw his love for me.

"I miss you and I love you," he said softly. "It may take some time, but if you're up for it, I want to try to make this work. I believe that you're moving forward and I'm so happy for you. I really appreciate what you just told me. I want to be honest with you, though—I'm worried you packing the clothes was just because I walked out."

I nodded. "I understand, and you know what? You leaving *was* part of the reason. It's something I've been wanting to do, but you walking out gave me that extra push I needed. But no matter what prompted it, the result is what matters most. I know I haven't made things easy for you. You've never asked me to do anything I wasn't ready for. I decided when it was time to take off my wedding rings, I decided when to say "boyfriend," and I took down photos when I was ready. All I can tell you is that now—like all those other times—I'm a hundred percent sure that I'm ready."

With a slow, happy smile, Arash pulled me into his arms.

*   *   *

Despite our brief detour away from each other, within days Arash and I were closer than ever. No longer on different roads, we were now walking toward the future together. A weight had been lifted from both of us.

Time healed Arash's doubts, proving to him that I meant what I said. I'd let go of the past. Yes, it would always be a part of who I was, but it didn't determine my fate. The past had broken me and rebuilt me into a newer, stronger version of myself. And now the future was calling my name.

After a year and a half of dating, Arash moved into my townhouse. With no more fears about our life together, that step was an easy one. As more time passed, we discussed marriage. My knee-jerk reaction was uncertainty—not of Arash, but of whether I wanted to get married again. The more we spoke about it, however, the more comfortable I was with the idea. But I made it clear that it wasn't something I absolutely needed. For me, it was enough that we were serious about our relationship and wanted to be together forever. We also spoke about starting a family, and came to a mutual conclusion that we wanted to have a child first and get married after.

*   *   *

On a beautiful morning in June, I took my morning coffee onto my deck to enjoy the lush trees and bird songs. I felt peaceful and happy as I reflected on how much my life had changed in a few short years. I couldn't wait to start a family with a wonderful man I loved dearly. But I was also aware of another urge. I wanted to visit Eddie and ask for his blessing. I needed a sign that he approved I was moving on.

About a month later, I returned to Chittenango. As always, on my way into town I stopped by the cemetery. I sat with Eddie for a while in silence, absorbing the deep peace of the place. Looking at the rendering of his smiling face, I finally told him about what had happened since I last visited. I told him all about Arash and how happy I was that we were planning to start a family. As best as I could through tears, I explained that I was ready for this next step and wanted him to be happy for me. The admission brought more tears.

"I need to know that you're okay, Eddie. I don't want to hurt you. I've been depressed for so long, and I've finally found happiness again. You will always be a part of me—I'll always love you. But I can't keep living in the past. Arash is a great man. He's been there for me through so much. He's shown me how to love again. I think we were brought together for a reason, and maybe you had something to do with that. Please, give me a sign. Anything. Please, somehow, show me that you're happy for me."

My only answer was the wind, blowing gently through the silent cemetery. I should have remembered that time obeys no one. I wanted an irrefutable sign from the universe right then and there, but I had to wait.

When the sign came three months later, it was in the form of a phone call from Finny. It began with, "I don't want to upset you, but I wanted to talk to you about something."

Oh geez, here we go, I thought to myself. Bracing myself for news that someone was in the hospital, or another reporter was looking for me for an interview, I quickly asked, "What is it?"

"Remember Rachel, who was friends with Eddie?"

"Yes, I do."

"Well, she was going through a hard time recently after the death of her aunt and decided to see a medium. She, um, reached out to me and Carson because, well, the medium apparently had a message for you."

Definitely not what I'd been expecting.

"What kind of message?" I asked hesitantly.

"You know how I don't really believe in psychics, but I didn't want to keep this from you. It was supposedly a message from Eddie. I don't know what it all means, but do you want to read it? Rachel wrote it all down and emailed it to me."

My hesitation vanished. "Yes, absolutely. Are you sending it now?"

"Just did. Take your time."

"Okay, I'll read it, then call you back." Ending the call, I opened my email and devoured Rachel's words.

I wrote down everything I can remember, and as much verbatim as I could. It started when the woman asked me, "Who's the soldier?" I told her my fiancé was a Navy vet and she said, "No no, this one is in spirit . . . Afghanistan, right? Second tour?"

So right off the bat, I knew she meant Eddie. Then she asked, "Who's Andrew/Andy? Something like that?" and I told her, "His wife's name is Andrea." She just smiled and said, "Yes, that's it."

She then went on to tell me, "There's a lot of anger surrounding his death, a lot of 'whys'. Mostly, though, it sounds like Andrea didn't want him to go on his second tour. The soldier wants Andrea to know that she was the wife she promised she would be, and he is so grateful for that. He also says that it's okay for her to move on. Specifically, he says he doesn't want her to lose her chance at having children, and that yes, on earth he would have been jealous, but in spirit he is not."

She also mentioned dog tags being wrapped around someone's hand or something, and that there is something very significant about his dog tags. And a baby, either lost or not born yet. I'm not sure what any of this means, but knew I should write it down. Hopefully it means something to Andrea."

I reread the email over and over, crying and laughing. My sign from beyond had come, after all. Rachel and I weren't close. She knew very little about my life and nothing at all about my plans with Arash. This was Eddie's doing. One last time, he'd come through for me.

I closed my eyes and whispered, "Thank you Eddie. Thank you for your blessing."

When I called Finny back, I explained how Eddie had answered my questions. Finny knew Arash and I had been talking about starting a family, but he didn't know about my conversation with Eddie at the cemetery. No one knew about my tearful plea for a sign from him. I'd loaned Diana Eddie's dog tags to wrap around her bouquet when she got married. She told me that carrying them gave her strength and surrounded her with his presence.

Finny was mystified, and I was ecstatic.

*   *   *

On the fourth anniversary of Eddie's death, I woke up with a feeling I never had before. In addition to my hatred of what that date represented, I felt odd. Different. While I had no physical symptoms, I knew what was happening. I was pregnant. Despite my curiosity, I held off on taking a test. The day belonged to Eddie.

The following morning which ironically happened to be Veteran's Day, I kissed Arash goodbye and he headed to work. Then I took a pregnancy test. I didn't have to wait long for confirmation—within seconds a vibrant, pink plus sign appeared.

Joy. Gratitude. Excitement. So many emotions flowed through me as I ran to the store to find a quick gift for Arash who'd be home in just a few hours for lunch. I bought a children's book and a magnet saying *I love my daddy*, and put them in a small box with the positive pregnancy test. With everything wrapped, I waited impatiently for him to arrive. It was torture not texting him immediately, but the result was worth it. I'll never forget the surprise and elation on his face when he opened the gift.

On a getaway to Turks and Caicos before the birth of our daughter, Arash proposed. He'd been acting oddly all day, checking our dinner reservations multiple times like he was worried they'd been cancelled. His mind was elsewhere and he was uncharacteristically fidgety. I shrugged off the behavior, privately amused by his fixation.

That evening, when we arrived at the restaurant, the hostess led us away from the dining area toward the beach. When she pointed to a secluded table set for two before the tranquil ocean, I turned in shock to Arash. He wore a satisfied grin.

After finishing a delicious meal against the backdrop of a spectacular sunset, Arash told me how happy he was with our life. "I couldn't imagine my life without you, Dre. If there's one thing you could change in our relationship, what would it be?"

Looking into his eyes, I said truthfully, "I wouldn't change anything. I'm so happy."

He smiled. "Well, to make our relationship more official, why don't we put it in stone?" From his pocket, he removed a stunning cushion cut diamond ring. "Will you marry me?"

Happy tears filled my eyes. "Yes."

*   *   *

On July 10, 2015, we welcomed our daughter, Kayla Rose, into the world. Arash and I discovered together that we could not envision any greater love. Holding her for the first time imprinted a moment inside us for the rest of our lives—an indelible flash of perception and appreciation.

Another such moment came a year and a half later. On the beach in Punta Cana in the Dominican Republic, our friends and families gathered around us. Our beautiful little girl wore an ivory-lace dress and flowers in her hair as she walked down the aisle with Diana. Finny stood at the white podium in the beautifully decorated gazebo, waiting to marry us, a smile beaming across his face. Even before I made the first step with my father, I could see tears in Arash's eyes.

I now pronounce you   *My family.*
man and wife,
February 10, 2017.

There was no hesitation on my part, no doubt or fear as I walked happily toward the man who completely changed my life. The man who gave me more than he would ever know. A second chance at life and love. A chance for a family and happiness.

My battle with time was over. The past was at peace, and the future was out of my hands. I was finally, irrecoverably immersed in the present.

And I was going to stay there.

Widow. The word that had captured my identity was no longer in control. I became a better version of myself using my struggles to see the good in people and the beauty in the world. Who are you calling a widow? I'm so much more than that!

THE END

AFTERWORD

I spent a lot of time drowning in my pain. I wouldn't say, however, that the time was wasted. I needed that time to grieve and cry, scream and hate the world. I needed to completely fall apart before I could figure out how to put myself back together.

I didn't figure it out alone. The tremendous support from my family and friends helped me get through each and every day. No matter how many times my depression caused me to push people away, there were many who stood firm at my side. They were my anchors while the storm of grief raged.

Grief is an intimate process, one that varies from person to person. In many ways it's intimate and impossible to explain to others. My struggle with strangers invading my life with probing questions or insensitive commentary remained ongoing throughout my process. In my experience, my grief seemed to bring insensitive and self-centered people out of the woodwork. To this day, I'm still stunned by some of the asinine comments and questions I received.

In nearly every instance, I stayed silent and accepted the abuse. Looking back, I wish I'd cared less about coming off as mean or abrupt. I wish I'd defended myself more, had firmer boundaries and responses. With my humor twisted by grief, I used to fantasize about being a black widow spider. She, at least, could protect herself. Only driven to bite when her web was disturbed, the black widow became a symbol of courage for me. I admired how she unapologetically protected herself.

In the end, though, the people that allowed selfishness to overwhelm their common sense and compassion only made me stronger. And while anger often overtook me, at times clouding my views on the world, I see more clearly now. I know that the majority of comments weren't directed at me in a malicious way, but came from a place of concern. When faced with someone else's tragedy, many people simply don't know what to say or how to act. *Should I give them space, or do they want me there? Do they want to talk about it, or should I talk about something else?* Unfortunately, there's no rulebook, and if there was, its contents would vary for each person and situation. Letting go of my anger has been another process, one I'm glad to say I've completed.

By no means am I attempting to speak for all military widows. Although we share the commonality of having lost a spouse in combat, I don't presume to know anything about their private experiences. I do, however, understand their pain—the anger, the terrible lack of closure, and the long-term emotional scars. I also know that these women are some of the most resilient, courageous people in the world.

The pain of losing a person you love never goes away. It becomes a part of who you are. But what you make of that pain is up to you. For a long time, my pain pulled me down and controlled my life. Now I use it as motivation to be a better person and to live my life as Eddie would have lived his. In keeping with his outlook on life, I focus on taking time to enjoy the little things, to dance and sing at the top of my lungs no matter how ridiculous I look, to smile through the tears, to laugh so hard that my stomach hurts, and to love. To love with every ounce of my heart.

The world can be a dark and uncertain place, but if you allow yourself to look beyond the tragedies, you'll see the good just waiting to be recognized. With all the varied experiences life brings, the most defining, compelling, and powerful experience of all is love.

It took me more than six years to finish writing my story. There were days I would write for hours, then months in which I didn't even want to think about it. There were so many times I contemplated deleting it all. Reliving the events described was torture, and yet, doing so gave me an avenue for deeper healing and catharsis. In these pages, I'm reminded of how far I've come. How strong I truly am.

My life today is both wonderful and real. I have a loving, supportive partner and a beautiful daughter who brings us more joy than we thought possible. I look at the world differently. It's not all darkness and depression, and neither is it all rainbows and butterflies. It's baby steps, deep breaths, and valuing each present moment.

Eddie will always be a part of me. I know that wherever he is, he's still pushing me and guiding me on my darker days. But I'm so grateful to have a second chance. A second chance at love, a second chance at happiness, and a second chance at having a family of my own. WWED—*What Would Eddie Do?* He'd smile that big, joyful smile and tell me how proud he is of me.

Dumb Shit People Say

(FROM THE JOURNAL OF ANDREA PEREZ)

This chapter is what originally motivated me to write this book and share my story. I was constantly bombarded with questions and remarks that were ignorant and hurtful. I was hesitant about including this chapter, fearing it would come off as too harsh. But I have come a long way and realize people mean well. At the time, my grief was raw and in my face. It took over and I would freeze up, unable to speak. When feeling doubtful if I should share this, many said I should be honest with how I was feeling at the time. That it's an important part of my journey and frankly, people need to hear it. So here it is!

*   *   *

Disclaimer: It's hard to know what to say to someone who's suffered a recent loss. I get that. That's why this list is a necessary one.

Consider this a public service announcement—a friendly reminder to think before you speak when approaching someone who's grieving.

223

Be kind. Consider how you might feel if the circumstances were reversed.

And if you don't know what to say? It's probably best to say nothing at all.

The list that follows, although not exhaustive, is a collection of some of the most typical, insulting, and off-the-wall comments and questions that I've received.

I've also included my own (unvoiced) replies.

*　　*　　*

He's in a better place.
Like where? Disneyland?

I truly understand what you're going through. I recently suffered a similar loss when injury took lacrosse away from me.
Sorry I missed the funeral. It must have been a tearjerker.

God only gives us what we can handle.
So if I was weak, my husband wouldn't have died?

I know how you feel, my Grandma died six years ago.
It's definitely difficult to lose anyone, but wasn't your grandma eighty-five?

Are you having an affair with my husband?
Your husband calling to check on me doesn't mean we're having an affair. You are delusional and crazy!

How are you coping? Are you seeing a therapist?
I have literally no idea who you are.

Aren't you the girl whose husband died?

Can you say that louder, please? Not enough people are staring at me.

How do you know Eddie?

You're at his funeral and you didn't bother to find out who his wife is?

Are you dating anyone?

Well, since you asked, I did get a few numbers at my husband's funeral ONE FREAKING MONTH AGO.

I'm so annoyed I have to spend the entire weekend with my husband.

I just buried my husband. I'd give the world to spend one more minute with him.

You're young. You'll meet someone else.

So since I'm young, I shouldn't mourn my husband's death? I should just forget about him and jump back into the dating pool?

I don't know what I would do if anything happened to my wife.

You're an asshole.

I don't know how you do it!

Well I don't have a choice, now do I?

Everything happens for a reason.

I'd really like you to explain to me what that reason was.

Only the good die young.

1. You're not Billy Joel.

2. Are you implying that we're not good because we're still here?

I feel bad for you.

I'm not looking for your pity!

You're Edward's widow!

Andrea. My name is Andrea.

✳   ✳   ✳

When you come face to face with someone who is grieving and feel the need to say something, keep it simple. Here are several comments I always appreciated:

I'm sorry for your loss.

If you say it from the heart, it's more than enough.

Please let me know if you need anything.

Chances are I probably won't ask. But if you're sincere, thank you.

What was Eddie's favorite sports team?

I appreciate people wanting to learn more about him and I enjoy talking about him.

I'd like to make a donation in Eddie's name. Where should I do that?

It means a lot when people want to help carry on his memory.

Eddie was a great man. He will truly be missed.

It's short, sweet and true.

We are so grateful for his sacrifice.

It's meaningful because it shows an understanding and respect that he was fighting for our freedom.

*   *   *

Acknowledgments

Without the love and support from my amazing family and friends, I would not be where I am today. Thank you to those who stayed by my side when I was at my worst. Thank you to everyone who encouraged me to find happiness again. And a big thank you to my friends, who encouraged me to write my story down.

Diana, you are my person. You are more than a sister, you are my best friend. Thank you for our late night phone calls, for allowing me to cry and shout when I needed it, and even more for the laughter. You know what I'm thinking just by looking at me and you are my voice of reason. Thank you for spending countless hours helping me edit and making sure my timeline was accurate. I would not be where I am today if it wasn't for you. I love you more than words can say.

Thank you to my incredible family and my supportive, loving parents for being there for me and guiding me every step of the way. I have grown to be the person I am today because of you. You taught me to never give up and work hard for what you want. Family is everything! I know in my heart that we will always be there for each other no matter what life brings.

A huge thank you and hug to my incredible editor Laura Halloran. I feel we were meant to connect. You have helped me transform my book into something I am proud of. Your patience and kindness helped me come out of my shell. Not only did you provide me with your immense talent, but also your friendship. You went above and beyond and I will forever be grateful to you!

Thank you Nicole Hartney, from Letter-eye Editing for taking my vision and story to a new level. You really understood with compassion what I'm trying to accomplish. I'm grateful for your honesty, hard work and thoughtful feedback.

Thank you to my fantastic beta readers Monika Bak, Terri Mertz, and Hache L. Jones for your time, your feedback and for your kindness.

Melina, I can't thank you enough for taking my vision for my cover photo and making it more than I could ever imagine. I'm so grateful for our friendship and your talent.

Thank you to my military friends. You were brought into my life by chance and very quickly became family. I will forever cherish our time together at Fort Polk, as well as the memories we've made since.

Thank you to the individuals throughout the years who have reached out to me and shared the personal difficulties you were struggling with. Your powerful stories continued to motivate me to write and share my story.

And finally, thank you to my husband Arash for encouraging me to write my story. Thank you for being my biggest supporter and believing in me when I didn't believe in myself. Your love made me whole again. You've given me a life I didn't think was possible and I'm grateful for you each and every day. I love you!

MILITARY SUPPORT FOUNDATIONS

One of the most common questions I receive to this day is what people can do to honor Eddie and support the men and women still fighting for our freedom. There are many wonderful organizations out there that help our active military, veterans, as well as the family members of those who don't make it home.

We owe a great deal to our service men and women who selflessly put their lives on the line for our freedom. Even after returning home from war, veterans and their families still need a lot of help. Some struggle with severe PTSD, depression, and/or physical disabilities. Below are some organizations that many may not know about.

Homes for Our Troops
https://www.hfotusa.org

Homes for Our Troops (HFOT) is a privately funded 501(c)(3) nonprofit organization that operates nationwide, building and adapting custom homes for severely injured post 9/11 veterans to enable them to rebuild their lives.

Operation Homefront
www.operationhomefront.org

Operation Homefront is a national 501(c)(3) nonprofit organization whose mission is to build strong, stable, and secure military families so they can thrive—not simply struggle to get by—in the communities they have worked so hard to protect. For over fifteen years, they have provided programs that offer: RELIEF (through critical financial assistance and transitional housing programs), RESILIENCY (through permanent housing and caregiver support services), and RECURRING FAMILY SUPPORT programs and services throughout the year that help military families overcome the short-term bumps in the road so they don't become long-term chronic problems.

Special Operations Warrior Foundation
http://specialops.org

The Special Operations Warrior Foundation ensures full financial assistance for a post-secondary degree from an accredited two or four-year college, university, technical, or trade school, and offers family and educational counseling, including in-home tutoring, to the surviving children of Army, Navy, Air Force and Marine Corps special operations personnel who lost their lives in the line of duty. The Special Operations Warrior Foundation also provides immediate financial assistance to severely wounded and hospitalized special operations personnel.

Fisher House
https://www.fisherhouse.org

Fisher House Foundation is best known for a network of comfort homes where military and veterans' families can stay at no cost while a loved one is receiving treatment. Fisher House Foundation also operates the Hero Miles program, using donated frequent flyer miles to bring family members to the bedside of injured service members as well as the Hotels for Heroes program using donated hotel points to allow family members to stay at hotels near medical centers without charge.

Pat Tillman Foundation
http://pattillmanfoundation.org

The Pat Tillman Foundation invests in military veterans and their spouses through academic scholarships—building a diverse community of leaders committed to service to others. The scholars chosen show extraordinary academic and leadership potential, a true sense of vocation, and a deep commitment to create positive change through their work in the fields of medicine, law, business, education, and the arts.

Paralyzed Veterans of America
www.pva.org

Paralyzed Veterans of America, a congressionally chartered veterans service organization founded in 1946, has developed a unique expertise on a wide variety of issues involving the special needs of their members—veterans of the armed forces who have experienced spinal cord injury or dysfunction.

Hope for Heroes Foundation
https://heroeshope.org

Hope for Heroes provides our nation's disabled heroes with an opportunity to restore a healthy, active lifestyle despite having suffered debilitating injuries while serving our country. Connecting with nature through outdoor pursuits assists our heroes in creating a sense of empowerment that impacts their daily life and overall well-being. Their trips and outings provide a sense of healing, personal accomplishment and bonding for heroes, caregivers, family and friends.

American Widow Project
www.americanwidowproject.org

The American Widow Project recognizes the sacrifices made by the families of our fallen and believes that no military widow should feel alone in her grief. Every military widow deserves the opportunity and tangible tools available to help rebuild her life. Because of that, the American Widow Project provides the vital peer-to-peer, emotional, and educational support necessary to maximize success, healing and hope for a brighter future.

ABOUT THE AUTHOR

Andrea Perez became a military widow at the age of twenty-five. Several years later, she began journaling as a form of therapy.

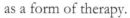

While she uncovered truths about herself, she simultaneously discovered a story with the power to help others.

Andrea loves working with children and carries out that passion working as a school counselor. She enjoys sports, outdoor activities, yoga, reading and spending time with her beautiful family and dog, Fred. Being a mom is her most precious gift.

Made in the
USA
Lexington, KY